Dancing till dawn broke

An anthology of poems

Parkinson's
Disease Society

Dancing till dawn broke

An anthology of poems

Published by
The Parkinson's Disease Society of the United Kingdom
22 Upper Woburn Place
London
WC1H 0RA

Registered Charity No. 258197
A company limited by guarantee
Registered No. 948776
Registered Office : 22 Upper Woburn Place
London WC1H 0RA

ISBN 0 -9530233 -0 -3

First published 1997

Typeset, Printed, and Bound in Great Britain by
The Lazarus Press
6 Grenville Street
Bideford
Devon EX39 2EA

  RECYCLED PAPER

Foreword

Three years ago I had the pleasure to meet Hilary Claydon who was diagnosed with Parkinson's in 1987, and during our meeting the idea of the anthology *Dancing till dawn broke* was born. I was immediately impressed by Hilary's sense of humour and bravery in coming to terms with this challenging illness; such as writing children's books of verse, three of which she has written, published and marketed. She also works very hard raising considerable funds to help others living with Parkinson's and their families.

During the years I have worked with the Parkinson's Disease Society of the United Kingdom, I have become increasingly aware of the creativity that exists within people who live with Parkinson's. The Society decided it would like to publish an Anthology of Verse, written by people affected by this illness and a request was published in the Society's 'Branch Bulletin' in July 1994, for people to send in poems. The results are contained within this book and Hilary, in her inimitable style, subsequently raised the funds for its publication. The Society extends a very sincere 'thank you' to this amazing woman.

Unfortunately, it has not been possible to publish all the poems received but I sincerely hope that all who read *Dancing till dawn broke* will enjoy the contents and applaud all those people who responded to our request.

Mary G Baker, MBE
National and International Development Consultant
Parkinson's Disease Society of the United Kingdom

For Myself
I knew as soon as I could read and write
That I must be a poet. Even today,
When all the way from Cambridge comes a wind
To blow the lamps out every time they're lit,
I know that I must light up mine again.

Taken from Summoned by Bells by Sir John Betjeman
Used by kind permission of John Murray (Publishers) Ltd

Contents

Contents

Contents

Contents

Contents

About this Anthology

The panel who compiled this anthology read through more than 500 poems before making their final selection. It was a hard decision to make, as each person differs in their taste for poetry. However, the sessions spent reading through the poems were extremely enjoyable and we hope you like the final selection as much as we do. The criteria used by the panel was *poems that speak to us*. We would like to extend thanks to all those who contributed a poem for the anthology, and to the Parkinson's Disease Society of the United Kingdom (PDS) for the privilege of being involved in the selection process.

The four members of the panel each had an association with Parkinson's and the PDS:

Robert Bogue has wide experience in theatre, films, and in training performers for the stage and television. Earlier in his career, his playwriting attracted ATV Network. More recently, he has had poetry published and was delighted to be asked to adjudicate on the panel to select poetry submitted by people associated with Parkinson's. Robert is a carer for his wife who has Parkinson's.

Hilary Claydon became involved in the anthology at the concept stage, and helped to raise money towards it. Hilary was diagnosed with Parkinson's in 1987. She has written, published and marketed three books of children's verse: *Here lies a tail or two*, *Safari rhymes for Windsor Safari Park*, and *Two by Two to London Zoo* (which was written to help London Zoo in their fight against closure). She tries in all her poetry to keep a sense of humour as this helps in the fight against Parkinson's.

Bridget McCall is Information Manager at the PDS and has worked for the organisation for nine years. She is an illustrator in her spare time and has provided designs for Christmas cards and children's books. One of her illustrations appears as the front cover of this anthology. Bridget enjoys literature and poetry.

Sarah Masters is Publications Manager for the PDS, co-ordinating a wide range of publications as well as the quarterly newsletter of the organisation. She writes fiction in her spare time and appreciates how hard it is to find a voice with which others can truly identify.

About the poets

F Ball was born on 28th September 1935. He served for four years in the Grenadier Guards, was married in 1958 and is the father of three children. After 23 years' service with West Midland Fire Brigade he was diagnosed with Parkinson's in 1985.

Robert Bogue has wide experience in theatre, films, and in training performers for the stage and television. Earlier in his career, his playwriting attracted ATV Network. More recently, he has had poetry published and was delighted to be asked to adjudicate on the panel to select poetry submitted by people associated with Parkinson's. Robert is a carer for his wife who has Parkinson's.

Mary Kathleen Brooke was born in Leicester in 1921 and was a lover of poetry and prose while still at school. Her work *A Personal Story* was published in *The Parkinson* in 1994, and a short comical sketch was written for her local *Town's Womans Guild*. Mary is a widow and as well as coping with Parkinson's, learning to play the organ and looking after her home, is currently writing her memories of World War II following a request by her grand-daughter.

Tim Clarke was born in Liverpool in 1922. He flew with the RAF during the last war and worked in the telecommunications industry until 1983. He was diagnosed with Parkinson's in 1990 and is the present Chairman of Liverpool Central Branch of PDS. Tim has written over 100 poems, many short stories, two novels and story-lines involving Parkinson's for various TV productions. As a result of an appearance on BBC's *The Travel Show* he has written a guide book *Exploring Anglesey*, and subsequently formed his own travel book publishing company.

Hilary Claydon became involved with this anthology at the concept stage, and helped to raise money towards it. Hilary was diagnosed with Parkinson's in 1987. She has written, published and marketed three books of children's verse: *Here lies a tail or two*, *Safari Rhymes for Windsor Safari Park*, and *Two by Two to London Zoo* (which was written to help London Zoo in their fight against closure). She tries in all her poetry to keep a sense of humour as this helps in the fight against Parkinson's.

Chris Coulson was born at Westminster, London, in 1948 into a Spiritualist family and *'would have been a true cockney except that the Bow Bells were down because of the war'*. Chris is currently writing an autobiography and has previously been published in YAPMAG. Chris is a registered medium with the Institute of Spiritualists & Mediums.

James Culwick was born in 1911, the younger son of a rector in the Church of England. He trained for the ministry, became a priest in 1935 and resigned his Orders four years later. James then pursued a varied career and lived with his wife in Hove from the 1960s. He later developed Parkinson's and died in 1990. Always keen to converse and communicate, in his last years his poems became ever more important to him.

Vina Curren was born in Chorley, Lancashire, in 1931 and is married with one son. Diagnosed with Parkinson's in 1991, Vina has been Lay Minister of Chorley Unitarian Chapel since 1988.

Hazel Cuthbertson was diagnosed as having Parkinson's in 1989 and, along with her husband John, is an active fundraiser and a strong believer in raising public awareness of Parkinson's through social contact. She has two daughters and three grand-children. Before developing Parkinson's, Hazel was a keen traveller and National Trust enthusiast and has latterly developed a strong interest in puzzle solving, scrabble, reading and writing. Her poem *The Patch*, chosen for this anthology, is her first work published.

Sylvia Davidson was born in South Wales in 1927, the daughter of a forrester. She was educated in Herefordshire and Reading and after a year at Domestic Science College she went to train as an occupational therapist, where she met her husband. For 30 years Sylvia worked as a wife and mother – for a time in North Carolina USA and in South Africa. Her lifelong interest in literature has led to her writing poetry and *Oh Joy! Oh Joy*! and *Snow* are her first published works.

Pat Dunn became ill with Parkinson's eleven years ago and has had four previous works published, among them S*eek the Lord and His Strength* in an anthology in 1994. Born in Liverpool in 1924, she was educated at the Everton Valley Convent High School. She has been married to her husband Hugh since 1947 and they have four children and four grandchildren. During the war Pat served with the War Office.

Rev. Colin Evans was born in Merthyr Tydfil and spent the years 1947-49 as a Sergeant in the Royal Army Educational Corps. He was part of an experimental touring theatre unit – along with his friend the late Brian Redhead – which proved an inspiration for one of Colin's four books *Reflections of a Stage-Struck Vicar.* From 1950 until retirement he was a minister within the United Reformed Church and contributed to broadcasts on Anglia & Southern TV and BBC Radio 2 & Radio 4. Married for 46 years to Margaret, they have four children and ten grandchildren and currently live in Suffolk.

Peter D Gray was born in Streatham in 1927 and completed his National Service in Northern Ireland and Egypt during 1945-48. He was an internal auditor before retiring in 1985 due to Parkinson's, and moving to Lincoln in 1989. He has one daughter and three grandchildren. Peter's hobbies are philately, listening to classical music, and playing carpet bowls with his local Parkinson's Disease Society group. His poem *I'm the lucky one*, chosen for this anthology, is his first published work.

Mary Henley was born in Portsmouth and educated at Bristol University. She has three children and five grandchildren. Mary was widowed in 1964 and remarried in 1978. She now lives in Bridport in Dorset and was diagnosed as having Parkinson's in 1989. She has since replaced her former hobbies of walking and gardening, with writing and painting. Her poem *Parkinson's Disease*, chosen for this anthology, is her first submitted for publication.

Margaret Hooper has lived all her life in Huddersfield. She has two sons and was widowed in 1987. Margaret was a private secretary but retired due to early onset Parkinson's at the age of 48. She writes the quarterly newsletter for her local PDS branch and is a member of YAPP&RS. Margaret has published a book of poems which helped raise funds for the PDS and has been published in various anthologies, magazines and the *Huddersfield Daily Examiner*.

Rosemary Jones at the age of five wrote a graphic description of a graveyard. She claims a schoolteacher told her she had 'too much imagination'! Her poem *Early One Morning*, chosen for this anthology is her first to appear in a book. Rosemary was diagnosed as having Parkinson's in 1988 and had to give up her work as a domestic co-ordinator at a local independent school. She lives in North Wales with her husband Owen. They have two grown up daughters.

Jennie Kendall was born in Bristol in 1943, married husband Jim in 1965, and has one daughter, Samantha. Jennie successfully ran her own hairdressing business for 21 years – ended by a delayed diagnosis of Parkinson's. She chairs her local branch of the PDS which she and other people with Parkinson's, started in September 1993. Offered the Chairship of South West YAPP&RS in June 1995, Jennie's life is now focused upon creating awareness of Parkinson's.

Anne S Limb was born in Ashover, Derbyshire in 1940 and worked for Chesterfield public library. Married to husband John in 1960, they have two children, Samantha and Carl. Anne was diagnosed as having Parkinson's just before her fortieth birthday. She is secretary of both the Chesterfield branch of PDS and YAPP&RS. Anne wrote her piece *Me and My Parkinson's* in 1988. This is her first published work.

Enid Long has been writing poetry for four years and has published three books of collected verse: *Collected Poems 1994*, *Under a Southern Sky*, and *Voices on the Wind*. Enid was born in 1938, is married to husband Ernest, and has one daughter and three grandsons. At present she lives in Bradninch in Devon and is disabled due to Parkinson's which she has had for 16 years. Enid underwent pioneering brain surgery in 1996 at Frenchay hospital in Bristol. However, a follow up operation was cancelled when the American machine, essential in the treatment, had to be returned to the USA.

Peggy Lowndes describes herself as a 'Pottery wench', having been born into a family involved in the pottery industry. As a mature student she gained a B.Ed (hons) degree and a teaching certificate. In 1981 she was diagnosed as having Parkinson's and had to give up her job as a reception teacher in 1990. Peggy states emphatically that she 'will not give in' and believes that Yoga helps her. She enjoys ballroom dancing, sailing, and playing the piano. She has been published in local newspapers, another anthology, and was until recently on the editorial committee of YAPMAG.

Ursula Madden is the author of *Clouds & Rainbows*, the auto-biographical book dealing with early-onset Parkinson's and its effect on her family. She was forced into early retirement from teaching due to Parkinson's and lives in Parbold, Lancashire with her husband Peter, who is a headmaster. They have four children. After mastering the use of a computer, Ursula has been published many times, and her short stories and poetry often reflect her sense of humour and strength of character.

Gordon Martin was a member of the Institute of Management Accountants when he retired in 1989 due to Parkinson's. He lives with his wife Maureen in Kirksandall, Doncaster and they have two sons. Gordon has had two poems '*Mine*' and '*World War III*' published in a book *Poets for Peace*.

Lynda McKenzie was born in Toronto, Canada in 1953, currently lives in Ontario, and has two children. She successfully ran her own craft business *Country Feelings* until she reluctantly had to sell due to the effects of Parkinson's, with which she had been diagnosed at the age of 34. After learning computer skills, Lynda realised she could transfer her love of crafting from 'stuffing and fabric' into 'words and stories'. She has since had five articles published in Canada.

Arthur Merrall was born in Salford in 1915 and graduated from Manchester University in 1937. He spent six years in the army from 1940-46, is married to wife Frances, and they have two daughters and four grandchildren. Arthur retired as a schoolmaster in 1977 and has been published previously by the *Poetry Institute*. He has had Parkinson's for six years.

Lynda Moreby spent part of her childhood in Singapore, and began training as a nurse in 1961 at the Canadian Red Cross Hospital at Taplow, later obtaining her SCM as a midwife. She is married and has one son, Paul. Lynda had worked for 18 years at Wokingham when she was diagnosed with Parkinson's in 1989. She was forced by ill-health to retire in 1990. Her poem *An Old Man* has been chosen for this anthology

Joan New was born in Rugby in 1931 and educated at Bedales School where her father was headmaster. She attended Exeter University and Birkbeck College. Joan retired in 1990 after a career in publishing (where she spent six years with *Which? Magazine*) and computer programming. Joan's husband was diagnosed as having Parkinson's in 1989. Her poem *A PD Rhyme* is Joan's first published work, though she has written lyrics for amateur musicals and cabarets.

Kees Paap was born in 1949 in the tiny village of Zandvoort, on the coast of Holland near Haarlem. In 1973 he married his wife Adrie by whom he has two children. In 1990 he was diagnosed as having Parkinson's and became a member of the Dutch *Parkinson's Patienten Vereniging* and was a founder member of the Dutch *Yoppers* and editor of their magazine. Latterly, Kees has initiated the EPNET (European Parkinson's Network) and PIBI (Parkinson's Information Bank International) and has written many poems on subjects such as life, love, Parkinson's, animals and humour.

Pamela Phillips was born in Leicester and moved to Suffolk at the age of ten. She has worked as a nursery teacher and is the mother of four married children. She has had Parkinson's for 15 years and was widowed five years ago. Pamela has been variously published in local village magazines and also in books. She states that she 'always tries to see the funny side of life' and will continue writing her beloved poetry while her health allows.

Janis Priestley lives with her husband in Litchfield and has three children. She has taught a wide variety of subjects in England and Zambia. Janis was diagnosed with Parkinson's in 1986, took retirement in 1990 and helped to found the Litchfield branch of PDS. Many of her poems and short stories have been published and she was shortlisted for the *Litchfield Prize* in 1991. Janis is a member of the *Society of Women Writers and Journalists* and the *Fellowship of Christian Writers*.

Margaret Randall a Londoner by birth, met her husband John as a pen-pal in the 1960s. She had excelled in writing before her early school years were abruptly ended when her father died and their home was destroyed in the Blitz. Although Margaret claims to have had a limited education, her success in having short stories, articles and poems published in various womens' magazines shows that she has made up for lost time. She enjoys writing about animals and what she calls *funnies*. 'Where would we be without our sense of humour?' asks Margaret.

Betty Robertson spent most of her early years living on a farm, which instilled in her a great love and repect for nature. Betty originally chose a career as a kindergarten teacher but in 1982 became a care assistant at a retirement home in Wensleydale. Early retirement was brought about by Parkinson's in 1984 and she later joined the Richmond (N. Yorks) Writers Group. Her first book *Stepping Stones* was published in 1996, and her second is due in 1997.

Diane Rule was born in Hampshire and was a departmental manager with the John Lewis Partnership before leaving to join her husband's business. She has two grown up sons. Diane was forced to give up work in 1992 due to Parkinson's and has since written nine poems. *Let it be*, chosen for this anthology, was her first poem.

Joy St Clair is a romantic novelist and short story writer whose work has been published worldwide. She was secretary of the Margate Chamber of Commerce for thirteen years and is currently a member of the *Society of Women Writers & Journalists*, the PDS, and judges the Joy St Clair annual romantic short story competition in aid of the PDS. Joy was married to Frank for 45 years and has a son and a daughter. She was diagnosed as having Parkinson's in 1985 and lives in a retirement home. Among her interests are cruising, playing keyboard, and 'spoiling her three grandchildren'.

Howard Stephens was married in 1968 and lives in Kenley, Surrey. He started writing at the age of 42, four years after being diagnosed as having Parkinson's. Howard won a writing competition in 1990, and has had two poems published nationally and many more in branch newsletters.

Hubert William Stuteley is 83 years old and has had Parkinson's for ten years. His poem *Overheard at the market* reflects his interest in the Suffolk dialect of his birthplace. Hubert has worked as a chauffeur and a valet in Sheffield but at the age of 21 returned to Suffolk to work on the land. He has had one other poem published. As well as writing, he enjoys whist, snooker and crosswords.

J Summers worked in India as a Missionary nursing sister for 17 years until ill health forced her to return to England. Invited by friends to live in Bristol, she began a new career caring for blind residents until diagnosed as having Parkinson's. In 1992 Miss Summers learned of St Monica Home, a very large and beautiful residential home – which specialises in caring for people with conditions like Parkinson's – originally endowed by the Wills tobacco family and situated on the edge of Bristol Downs. She now lives there, very happily, and her poem *Snowdrops at Candlemas* has been previously published in St Monica's quarterly newsletter.

Doris E Taylor was born in the 1920s and, despite a hip abnormality, enjoyed a happy childhood. She is married with one son and one grandaughter. At the age of 35 her hip disability worsened to the extent that she required the use of a wheelchair. Since this time, Doris has come through a period of resentment and frustration, followed by an acceptance of her condition, and has found an inner strength which has enabled her to learn to drive, to obtain a job, and to publish two books of poetry: *Precious Moments* and *More Precious Moments*. Doris is involved with spiritual healing and believes that this helps her enormously.

Bert Tolfrey was born Herbert William Tolfrey in Bolton in 1916. Bert spent his war years in the RAF, mostly in India, and worked for 32 years as an accountant. His wife died in 1993 and Bert has been 'aware of Parkinson's' since 1992. The father of three children and grandfather of two grandchildren, he has been a member of the *Songwriter's Guild* (now BASCA) since 1954 and the *Performing Rights Society* (PRS) since 1968. Bert has a catalogue of 300 musical items registered with PRS and has had six songs broadcast.

Edward Urry lives in Chelsfield, Kent, with his wife. They have three grown up children. Edward retired as a financial director in 1992 due to Parkinson's which was diagnosed nine years earlier. Edward has followed a varied career as an industrial chemist, accountant, and business analyst. Both he and his wife are active members of YAPP&RS and Edward spends a lot of his time writing and 'keeping the house tidy'. A previous work, *I suffer, who cares?* was published by Carers World.

Tara Vasudevan attends St Helenas School in Colchester. At the time of writing her poem, she was 12 years old. She wrote the poem on Non-School Uniform Day in November 1994, after participating in a poetry workshop run by Hilary Claydon, a poet who has Parkinson's.

Joyce Wicks was born in Harrow and has had Parkinson's for ten years. Her husband died in 1992. She has led a varied and interesting life, working for such institutions as Hoover, Kodak, British Telecom and The Department of Trade & Industry. Her interests, beside writing, are gardening and music. She is presently learning to play electronic keyboard. *Always Summer* is her first published work.

Spirituality

He laughed and called to them, 'Look at me!
I'm going to reach the sky!'
And reach the sky he did.

MOMENTS

Take each moment as they come,
Treat them gently, one by one;
Live each moment of each day
In love and harmony, and pray
That each one can be wisely spent
With no regrets, and no torment,
No aching hearts, no fears, no dread
To mar the next moment ahead,
For once gone, it will not provide
A second chance, but if you've tried,
You'll know the joy each moment brings
If you can only do the things
To make it so, and not forget
How wonderful they are – and yet –
It's up to you, to make each day,
The moments spent in such a way,
That everything you do is better
And complies with God's plan to the letter.
Treasure then, these moments rare,
Treat each one with loving care,
They are but a fleeting gem
So make it worth remembering them;
Let the past go, whether happy or sad,
Trust future moments will not be so bad;
Have faith in yourself,
Whatever the test,
Live just for each moment
And make it your best.

Doris E Taylor

TYRINGHAM

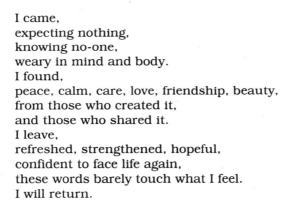

I came,
expecting nothing,
knowing no-one,
weary in mind and body.
I found,
peace, calm, care, love, friendship, beauty,
from those who created it,
and those who shared it.
I leave,
refreshed, strengthened, hopeful,
confident to face life again,
these words barely touch what I feel.
I will return.

                    Peggy Lowndes

ALWAYS SUMMER

To sit in some secluded place
And feel the sun upon my face,
To while away the hours
And hear the buzz of bees in flowers,
The leaves that rustle through the trees
Borne across the gentle breeze.
Blue skies
And dragonflies.
The birds that sing, just for the reason
That it is the summer season,
Oh, that it could constant be
Always summer time, for me.

Joyce Wicks

4

SEEK THE LORD AND HIS STRENGTH

A peaceful scene, a golden summer evening,
Dinner set out, the family gathered in.
The mother quietly pleased to set good fare before them
Sat down herself, prepared to eat her food.

The times were stressful for her and now and then
She had to fight her way through panic attacks,
Her husband always helping when he was at home.

But now the terror struck suddenly,
                    no time to seek his help
Or gather resources of her own.
She was falling, falling, into space. Or so it seemed.
Her very being, like two arms, stretched up,
                    beseeching aid,
And was grasped by Another, familiar as herself
                    and yet
Completely Other. Drawn up by Mighty Power
                    and gently placed in safety.
She was back, no time had passed, the family unaware.

                                        Pat Dunn

5

THE BRIDGE

Walking through this leafy glade,
I revel in tranquility,
My thoughts transcend from worldly cares
And peace is all around me.

The sunshine filters through the trees,
And as I pause, absorbing warmth,
A rustic bridge comes into view.

And now a silent question forms
Within my cleared mind,
Should I attempt to cross the bridge,
The more delights perhaps to find?
Or should I stay here
Where I am
And savour what I have?

How many more have trod this path
And faced this same dilemma?
Did they decide to cross the bridge
In search of further treasure?
Or did they opt like me to stay,
Afraid of what they'd find?

Perhaps one day
I'll cross the bridge
If courage can be found.
Till that day dawns
I shall remain
And keep what I have thus far gained.

Ursula Madden

CONSOLATION

Along the rough and stony road,
With failing heart and faltering step,
My lonely trek began.
The sun had left the darkened sky,
Potential dangers lurked
In gathering gloom.
Despair's cold fingers clutched
Around my heart and
In the desolate waste
Surrounding me
My eyes could find no exit,
No way out.
Panic surged within me,
Turning fast to empty numbness.

And then it was
With gentle touch,
You made your presence known,
You reached deep down within me
And released my anchor'd spirit.

Filled with new life
By the warmth of your love,
It soared above my troubled mind
And came to rest on Hope
As a butterfly on sunshine.

And thus, for now,
It shall remain,
Swaying on emotional breeze,
In fluttering anticipation
Of eventual solution.

                              Ursula Madden

7

TRANQUILITY

T —   for the texture of the clouds
       Billowy, soft and white
R —   for the rainbows making
       Arcs of colour in the sky
A —   for aroma of flowers and fruit
       Invading the atmosphere
N —   for the noise of leafy trees
       Gently swishing in the breeze
Q —   for the quest of wanderers
       Looking for something new
U —   for the undulating waves
       At the edge of a shimmering sea
I —   for the intricate patterns of shade
       Creating complex designs on the ground
L —   for the lightness of spirit we feel
       When the pressures of life are lifted
I —   for the insects and butterflies
       Which herald the onset of warmth
T —   for the tenderness of love
       Manifested in all its forms
Y —   for the yearly season of sun
       Encompassing all these joys

Ursula Madden

THROUGH MORE THAN FORTY YEARS...

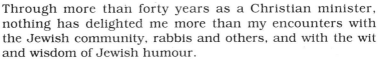

Through more than forty years as a Christian minister, nothing has delighted me more than my encounters with the Jewish community, rabbis and others, and with the wit and wisdom of Jewish humour.

One Saturday I joined an ecumenical party on a visit to the fashionable synagogue in St. John's Wood, situated opposite Lord's cricket ground. We were bowled over and knocked for six when the official at the door lightened the heavy formality of the occasion by remarking to us Christians, 'You will note that we are not on the Lord's side.'

In Buffalo, USA, I discovered that Hans Vigelund, the organist of Westminster Presbyterian Church, also played for the Friday evening and Sabbath services at the beautiful, brand new synagogue, Temple Beth Zion, not far down Delaware Avenue. The local rabbi, proudly showing us around and aware that everyone expects a Jew to be for ever doing deals like Lord Grade, said, 'How much will you give us for our new Temple?'

Back home, after leading one of several pilgrimage parties to the Holy Land and having written about it in my weekly column in the *Watford Observer*, I was invited to the Wembley synagogue to address the Tuesday men's meeting on the subject. They were on the brink of losing their rabbi, Dr Albert Friedlander, about to move into West London. During question time one member asked, 'Why don't you come and be our new rabbi?'

Taken aback, I explained that I was hardly qualified. 'All I can say,' I went on, 'is that I possess a much-cherished Jewish prayer book given me in America; oh, and I've been to see *Fiddler on the Roof*.' As speedily as Jehu in his careering chariot, my questioner cheekily wisecracked back, 'Mention those in your application!'

It must have been a Jew who remarked: 'I've got Parkinson's disease, and he's got mine.'

Colin Evans

THE MOUNTAIN BIKE SAMARITAN

Along the road to Dingle' O, there trudged a lonely man,
Carrying his heavy load, he did not own a van.
And as he walked by Otterspool,
                        cold was the night and dark,
The street lamp bulbs had all been smashed
                        as he approached the park.

Then in the distance far away,
                        some moving lights shone out.
And racing down the lonely road,
                        three bikers on their mounts.
They saw the lonely little man,
                        and quickly each one thought:
'He can't escape our motor bikes: he'll easily be caught.'

They chased him right along the road, 'til he exhausted fell.
They kept him lying on the ground:
                        and stole his load as well.
They revved their engines as they raced,
                        around and round about.
'Til he was sick with fear and dread
                        at every awesome shout.

They screamed with joy and revved and roared
                        their engines racing loud.
To someone lying on the ground it was a frightful sound.
And as they raced around and round
                        they lashed out with their feet,
The object of their hatred was white as linen sheet.

Soon on their bikes they jumped again,
                        and up the road they sped,
With never even a backward glance;
                        the poor man might be dead.
But not a care they had for him,
                        he'd been their evening sport,
It really had been his own fault, a lesson he'd been taught.

Our hero lying in the road was in an awful plight,
Not only had he lost his goods, he'd had a rotten fright.
The blood which poured out from his wounds
                    ran down into the dirt,
His clothes were torn, his head was cut
                    and every bone was hurt.

He must have lain for many hours,
                    while rats and foxes roam,
Close to him, sniffing at his blood,
                    as he just prayed for home.
'Twas many hours 'til daylight, he did not think he'd last
Unless a miracle occurred, and some kind soul came past.

A while after those lads had left, the road was full of light.
A Rolls Royce purred then into view,
                    all chrome and shining white.
But when the chauffeur saw the blood
                    upon the stranger there,
The High Priest signalled him to move,
                    for he was late for prayer!

And then there passed a few more hours;
                    our hero lay in pain,
Was almost giving up the ghost,
                    when he heard a noise again.
Another massive car came by, this time with business men.
As they had had a lot to drink, they all must stop again.

They went into the bushes, with not a glance around,
Nor even pity for him lying on the ground.
And when they all were comfortable
                    they got back in their car.
'We can't take any corpses, we've got to travel far.'

Well, after many painful hours, he saw another light,
Just like the flickering of a torch, it wasn't very bright.
A fellow on a mountain bike came down across the plain.
He hadn't bothered with the road,
                    he liked the rough terrain.
He stopped beside the traveller and chased the rats away,
He knew he could not leave him there
                    until the break of day.
He wiped some blood from off his face,
                    and bound his deepest cuts,
And looked round for shelter, but there were not even huts.

He gently lifted him across his pushbike's handlebars,
And pushed him slowly down the road,
                    beneath the twinkling stars
He wheeled the bike quite gently
                    and tried to miss the bumps,
And potholes in that unkept road
                    between the rubbish dumps.

So after several weary miles he came down to a pub,
Not just a common hostelry, it was an all night club.
Most of the staff had all gone home, there was not any din.
But a light was shining in the porch,
                    so there was someone in.

The cyclist knocked upon the door
                    which soon was opened wide,
The landlord roughly told him, 'Only members come inside.'
But when he saw the piteous state
                    in which they looked by now,
He took them in and kindly said,
                    'We'll manage him somehow.'

They put him on a comfy bed, and bandaged up his head.
'Look after him,' the cyclist unto the landlord said.
'I haven't got much money, but if you find it hard,
This number here should do the trick, it is my credit card.'

This parable will tell a tale, what happened to our Joe,
When he went out one pitch black night
                    on the road to Dingle' O.
The street lights were all out of course,
                    the bulbs had all been shot.
It is always dark and frightening in that Liverpudlian spot.

Who is the hero of this tale? Our poor and battered lad?
Or yet the mountain biker? But isn't it quite sad
To think that priest and businessmen
                    could still leave him to die?
But maybe p'raps that cyclist: – *Could he be you or I?*

                                        Tim Clarke

12

ETERNITY

Have you ever thought how it would be
To be a mighty great oak tree
To watch the centuries come and go
Since from when an acorn you did grow
How wise and patient you'd need to be to stand
The idiosyncrasies of man
Then you may have the merest glimpse of an idea
Of how you seem to us within the spirit sphere

Chris Coulson

GIVING

The moon gives us silver, the sun gives us gold,
And spring gives us flowers, forever to hold.
The moon gives us light, the sun gives us warmth,
And spring gives us hope, to help us go forth.

The moon gives us night, the sun gives us day,
And spring gives us youth, to go on our way.
The moon is the mystic, the sun is the king,
And spring is the child, that they both bring.

Like the moon and the sun, and spring with its joy,
You give me these gifts like jewels to enjoy.
Like the moon and the sun, and the spring like a dove,
I will treasure these gifts, for they are given with love.

Edward Urry

TRANQUILITY

The candle flame,
Slim and yellow,
Casts shadows
Of things we know
So well;
Weird shapes,
Yet somehow
Wistful.
Reminiscent
Of long ago.
Subdued light
Echoing tranquility;
A blessed
Peacefulness.
Quietly restful;
Soothing away
The trials of a
Busy day.
Time
Passes slowly
In candlelight.

Betty Robertson

THERE'S ALWAYS TOMORROW

There's always tomorrow
When today's not quite right,
There's always tomorrow, which
Could throw a new light
On a problem unsolved,
A problem that's made
A heart feel so heavy,
Turning sunlight to shade;
For so long it's allowed
The shadows too near,
This nagging, this doubting,
This worrying, this fear;
But think of today
As a cloud in the sky
Floating slowly but surely
On the breeze passing by;
Think only of beauty, be aware
It's no illusion,
Think of today,
And draw this conclusion:
There's always tomorrow
To think of today,
If things go awry,
Just throw them away;
Whatever our burdens,
Or problems, or sorrow,
Think only of Him,
There's always tomorrow;
Send Him your love
With your hopes and your fears,
Though He knows all your longings,
He sees all our tears;
But there's always tomorrow
If things aren't quite right,
There's always tomorrow,
So live in the light.
That's why we all are
Permitted to borrow
The knowledge He's given us,
There's always tomorrow

Doris E Taylor

16

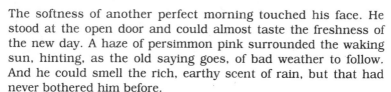

The softness of another perfect morning touched his face. He stood at the open door and could almost taste the freshness of the new day. A haze of persimmon pink surrounded the waking sun, hinting, as the old saying goes, of bad weather to follow. And he could smell the rich, earthy scent of rain, but that had never bothered him before.

Like a young sparrow perched on the edge of his nest, he savoured the thought of his outing for a minute or two. Then he was gone. Through his backyard, up over the sturdy wooden fence he had built many years before and over the laneway to the park beyond. He watched early risers walk their eager dogs and sleepily socialize. He watched the children on the swings as they pumped their legs and swung almost as high as they could dream. He couldn't remember the last time he had done that, so he joined them. Soon he too soared back and forth. Absorbed in their play, none of the children noticed the empty swing as it arched higher and higher.

He laughed and called to them, "Look at me! I'm going to reach the sky!"

And reach the sky he did. He sailed through the cotton clouds. He soared past sea gulls and swallows, dipped and climbed and soared again. The fresh morning breezes guided him over meadows filled with dancing spring flowers. He watched the town wake and stretch and come to life. He visited his favourite places; the giant oak tree where he had carved his initials and intertwined them with his sweetheart's, the dark mossy cave where he had stolen his first kiss, and the brook that bubbled under the wooden bridge where he and his son had fished.

Too soon it was time to return. Too soon he slowly made his way back to the room.

"Have you nodded off again, Mr Johnston? It's time for your morning walk! Here, let's get you comfortable...." The efficient little nurse adjusted the blanket around his knees and pushed the wheelchair towards the door. "Oh, dear, it's starting to rain. I had a feeling it might," she babbled on. "We'll just have to wait awhile for our outing, Mr Johnston. I hope you don't mind too much!"

Mr Johnston really didn't mind at all, for he had already been.

Lynda McKenzie

17

THE FLOOD

The rains lashed down, and soon the place was so flooded that the Christian had to climb up on to his roof, where he clung to the chimney stack and prayed earnestly to God to save him.

Soon a rubber dinghy came along, and the rescue crew shouted to him to get in with them.

'I am fine,' he replied. 'I am praying to my God and He will save me, you go and rescue more needy people.' So off the rubber dinghy went.

The waters rose still further until they reached his chest, when along came a lifeboat. The lifeboatmen shouted to the man to get in with them.

'I am fine,' he replied again. 'I am praying to my God and He will save me, you go and rescue more needy people.' So off sailed the lifeboat.

As the waters reached right up to his chin he saw a helicopter overhead, and the winchman shouted to him to join him on the rope.

'I am fine,' he replied yet again. 'I am praying to my God and He will save me, you go and rescue more needy people.'

So off the helicopter flew and the waters rose still further until, with a few dying bubbles, the Christian found himself facing God.

'Oh my God, why did you not try to save me when I prayed so hard to you?' asked the bewildered Christian.

'Not try to save you!' replied God, 'I sent a rubber dinghy, a lifeboat, and even my helicopter, and you would not get in any of them. What more did you expect me to do?'

Submitted by Tim Clarke

Community

'Ten minutes with the tea lady?'
He asked, a heartfelt plea.
'I promised her I'd visit when
I came this way, you see.'

DAWN CHORUS IN A HOSPITAL WARD

Such a grunting and a snoring,
Every bed does groan and shake.
Our dawn chorus, every morning,
Long before the birds awake.

Some are restless, some have nightmares,
Some on pills to ease their ache.
While the nurses do their night-cares,
Long before the birds awake.

Slowly as the windows lighten,
Staff arouses with a shake,
Takes our pulses, bedclothes tighten,
Long before the birds awake.

So again a new day breaketh,
Daylight floods in like a lake,
So a hospital awaketh,
And at last the birds awake.

Tim Clarke

SPECIALIST'S ROUNDS

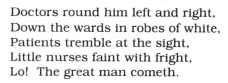

Doctors round him left and right,
Down the wards in robes of white,
Patients tremble at the sight,
Little nurses faint with fright,
Lo! The great man cometh.

Fast and fearless doth he stride,
And each bed he stops beside,
Juniors, questioned, glow with pride,
Patients told to "open wide",
Lo! The great man looketh.

Case sheets studied by each bed,
Ulcer vile or battered head,
"Intravenously fed".
"What was it his GP said?"
Lo! The great man speaketh.

Carefully examines all,
X-rays, pulse chart on the wall,
Nothing missed, however small,
Sister questioned at his call,
Lo! The great man questeth.

As his cohorts stand around,
Daring not to make a sound,
Wond'ring what the sage has found,
That will their poor brain astound,
Lo! The great man thinketh.

Diagnosis, then his plan,
"Operation, here we can".
"Fluids only, solids ban".
"Think we can discharge that man".
Lo! The great man judgeth.

Then he's passed the final cot,
Every malady did spot,
Out the end door goes the lot,
And the sister wasn't shot,
Lo! The great man leaveth.

Tim Clarke

21

TEN MINUTES WITH THE TEA LADY

The ward was hushed, the visitors
Had all turned tail and fled,
Staff and patients in F9
Had just prepared for bed;
When doors creaked open, in *he* crept,
A gentle little one.
The suit, well worn, was brushed and pressed,
The shoes buffed till they shone.
Hair combed back on balding head –
Smartness was his goal.
Fuchsias in abundance tumbled
From his buttonhole.
And in white-knuckled hand was clutched
A wonderful bouquet.
A hush fell on the ward as we
Prepared for what he'd say.
We gazed in silent wonder
As "Staff" stepped up and said:
"May I help you, sir?" he blushed,
A gentle shade of red.
"Ten minutes with the tea lady?"
He asked, a heartfelt plea.
"I promised her I'd visit when
I came this way, you see."
They'd met across the trolley whilst
He was ill in bed.
"I'll soon be in the ladies' ward
Myself," was what she'd said.

Aches and pains forgotten as we
Watched this one-act play.
The air was still and silent, then we
Heard the staff nurse say –
"I'm sorry, sir, the lady's gone –
She left some days ago".

His shoulders drooped, his eyes grew sad,
His gait became quite slow,
He sadly turned towards the door
As he prepared to leave.
I'm sure I'm not the only one
Whose tear fell on her sleeve!
His flowers seemed to wither as
He headed for the door,
A piece of fuchsia from his lapel
Fluttered to the floor.

Back to normal once again,
We climbed into our beds.
Lots of temperatures to take
And pills for aching heads.
I know we all had one more pain
Before we fell asleep.
The pain of love's 'old' dream, now lost,
A date he couldn't keep.
I'd like to leave a happy end,
But this I cannot do.
I'm sure he'll find his lady some day soon
If love is true.
And as I journey through my life
I'll ne'er forget that day.
"Ten minutes with the *tea lady*?"
Was all we heard him say!

                    Pamela Phillips

OH JOY! OH JOY!

Oh joy! Oh joy!
This is the day
My teacher comes to me!
Hurry up carer, don't be late and like to linger.
Get me ready early (clean dress today),
I want to be feeling my best.
Brush my hair and make it curly
– and lay two cups today, now in case he's early.
What is it today? Picts, Celts, Angles, Vikings?
I know a little,
            but hope that you know much much more!
Perk up brain cells,
            waste not a moment of this precious hour!

He's gone, but what did he say?
Oh yes, the tape.
            I can play that to my heart's content
And forget the imprisonment of wheelchair
And flights of steps and now my beloved's face,
Without whose care, time is but a waiting game.

                              Sylvia Davidson

I'M ONLY GOING TO THE CORNER SHOP

Have I got my list made out, and have I locked the back?
I'll take my umbrella, I might be glad of that.
I'd better put the cat out, I'm glad I thought of that –
I don't want to come back
     and find he's puddled on the mat.
I'd better turn the gas off, my saucepan burnt before.
Now I'm nearly ready, where's the keys to my front door?
I'd better put a coat on, it's turning rather chilly,
And I think I'll take a walking stick,
     that road up there is hilly.
Did I close the windows? Of that I must make sure,
I don't want to come back and find
     everything on the floor.
Where did I put my basket? I had it yesterday –
It must be in the cupboard.
     Which one? Did I hear you say.
I've found it, so I think I am almost ready
I've got my coat and got my stick,
     so now just take it steady.
I don't think I've forgotten just what I have to do,
I'm only going for a loaf of bread and jam and butter too.
Right, I'm off, it's not far up the street.
Oh dear, I've just remembered,
     my purse is indoors and I've slippers on my feet.

M.K. Brooke

THE SHORTHAND/TYPIST

As a typist I was always very fast –
In the speed tests I never came the last.
With shorthand I could speed along the line,
And when I typed it back it turned out fine.

But the day arrived when I had such a shock,
My hands were no longer steady as a rock.
My shorthand book, it trembled like a leaf –
My composure had been stolen by a thief!

I worried – does my boss think I'm afraid?
I dare not ask, to get my fears allayed.
So every time I went to take a letter,
I thought – he's sure to ask for someone better.

So You See My Dilemma

Back at my desk, with paper in machine,
I hope to type the nicest letter ever seen,
But I'm afraid that this was not to be –
My fingers would not co-operate you see.

I never had been one to make mistakes,
But suddenly my hands – they had the shakes.
The letter 'a' - it made me frown,
My little finger *could not* press it down!

The mechanic, he is needed here I think,
To put my typewriter back in the *pink*.
He studied all the parts with greatest care –
And seated himself down onto a chair.

'There's absolutely nothing wrong you know,
So now I'll put my coat back on and go.'
He left me with my face creased in a frown,
Why would that little key just not go down?

But matters, they did not improve at all –
Confidence in my ability began to pall.
Each morning I approached my job with fright,
I was nervous that my work would look a sight.

So You See My Dilemma

Each night after hours of sitting at my desk,
I went home just feeling like a wreck,
My entire body was so stiff and seemed to ache,
And once at home I just couldn't keep awake.

Of course at home I'd lots of things to do,
But I walked about as though I had the 'flu.
Everyone at home – they worried so,
But I knew that back to work I'd have to go.

I struggled bravely on, until one day
Dreadful problems quickly came my way.
My entire body was just wracked with pain.
I never thought that I would go to work again.

And I Didn't

The boss was understanding, he was great.
'I will not let you get into a state,
Go home and rest, and take it easy,
I can see that you are feeling really queasy.'

My resignation they just would not accept.
'I cannot write you off like this as yet –
Go back home and rest - I'll send a letter,
And when you read it you will feel much better.'

And I Did

So everyone was wonderful to me,
(At this time I did suspect it was P.D.)
I wanted my suspicions to be wrong,
Unfortunately for me and mine I was proved right.
On this occasion I would like to have been wrong!

Margaret Hooper

TO A FATHER ON HEARING THE TERMS OF HIS WILL

The scent of crushed rose petals from the kitchen floor
Evokes no sympathy anymore,
Browning and bruised, they still smell sweet,
Still feel like soft velvet beneath my feet.

The funeral over; the guests have grieved and left,
Leaving us feeling oddly alone and bereft;
Like strangers meeting outside the door,
Or friends with nothing left to say anymore.

Yesterday we spent preparing the cold collation,
It seemed only fitting for a man of your station.
The funeral tea was a really good spread,
A chance for everyone to speak ill of the dead.

Only today we learned the terms of your will.
Was your heart so full of hatred still?
None of us guessed you felt like that,
Leaving your wealth to the family cat.

We've swept the crushed rose petals from the kitchen floor,
For they won't be needed here anymore.
We threw them out with the household trash,
Next bonfire we have – they'll be like you – ash!

And when the cat dies there'll be no cold collation.
We're already planning a far grander celebration.
Till then he can snooze all day without care,
For no-one's bothered to tell him you made him your heir.

Janis Priestley

I'M THE LUCKY ONE

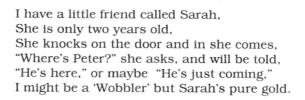

I have a little friend called Sarah,
She is only two years old,
She knocks on the door and in she comes,
"Where's Peter?" she asks, and will be told,
"He's here," or maybe "He's just coming,"
I might be a 'Wobbler' but Sarah's pure gold.

She doesn't notice that I am a 'Wobbler',
Or that I've frozen or feeling low,
She cheers me up and makes me laugh,
She does not worry if I am slow,
"Play on the floor, Peter," is her request,
Oh, I wish I could, that I know.

I have my wife to support me
And some very good friends as well,
So with them, and my little friend Sarah
I'm the lucky one – you can tell.
I can laugh at my *Faux Pas* with them,
Without them, I would miss them like hell.

My wife has written this poem,
She knows we are lucky too,
For the light of our lives, little Sarah,
Well, bless her she has not a clue,
I might be a 'Wobbler' to others,
But to Sarah I am still only two!

Peter D Gray

WHO IS COMING?

I wonder who is coming in today?
To visit me within this lonely ward,
Who'll brave the weather and too briefly stay,
And cheer me up and stop me getting bored.

Of course there is the thought that none may come at all,
The weather's foul with snow and fog about,
Buses are off and taxis may not call,
It isn't fit for folk to venture out.

Until the doors are opened, we'll not know
Who's braved the elements, till then we only guess,
And wonder who, if any, faced that snow,
To bring to me a smile, a kiss and a caress.

But every day we thank the Lord again,
For loving ones who use their evening hours,
Just coming here to ease our gloom and pain,
Bringing us love, and fruit and pretty flowers.

Tim Clarke

THE SPONSORED CHEWING GUM CHEWERS DAY

On the village shop they made a run
For the fattest sticks of chewing gum.
Very soon the shelves were bare;
Nothing but polished wood lay there.

The cash and carry was raided next.
Soon all remained was this little text:
'Reorder Now: You Need More Stock!'
But where could more chewing gum be got?

So back and forth across the town
They hunted gum both up and down.
Through every shop and house and drain
They searched once and twice, and yet again.

Could their sponsored chew begin that day?
Without sufficient gum was it fair play?
But at eight o'clock, whistles blew
And resolutely all began to chew.

As the autumn night slowly blackened,
Those chewing jaws drooped and slackened,
Until one by one the chewers slept
And only one small boy his promise kept.

Pack after pack he chewed and swallowed.
Spearmint, peppermint, closely followed
By lemon, lime, orange and berry
Finished off with a stick of cherry.

Questioned next day about the loss of gum,
He averred quite strongly – that thieves had come
While the said chewers were sound asleep,
Being awake he'd had a quick peep.

Now, we all know it is never wise
To swallow much gum nor yet tell lies;
For the child exploded, proving thus
That sponsored chews are ridiculous.

Janis Priestley

Memories

And dream again
Of dancing till dawn broke...

TIME (RETIREMENT??)

Time on my hands and dreams in my heart,
Days full of leisure, I ask – where to start?
So often I've said no time to do that,
And now time is plenty, I'm feeling quite flat.
I ask myself why I can't be up to my eyes
In unfinished jobs which I used to disguise;
Never a moment to think or to worry,
And days full of wishing to rest and not hurry!
Well, those days are gone, and time's all my own
And I sit here reflecting my memories alone;
But surely, I tell myself, now is the day
To get on with those hobbies I've got stowed away;
There's music, there's painting,
And sketching of trees,
There's time to sit listening
To the whispering breeze;
Time to watch nature and absorb all the love
Pouring forth from the flowers
And the mixed skies above.
There's so much to do
And to think of and plan –
In fact, my enthusiasm's got quite out of hand!
So today, here I sit, with nothing to do,
But who am I kidding,
Because that's just not true!
It's just that I think
It must sometimes be best
To have all this leisure
And dreaming and rest
Just stored away snug,
In the back of our minds –
To always look forward to
When nature unwinds.
Then time will blossom, and time will allow
Not only to use it but show us all how;
I ask just one thing –
To be able to share
The time to do nothing
With someone else there.

Doris E Taylor

THEN AND NOW

Remember tramping up that hillside
As you once did some years ago,
Into a breeze that surged around you,
Embracing gently the thrust of flesh,
Feet, legs, body taking the rise.
Past a sheep's skull, a memento mori,
A gaping grin from the edge of the path,
Mocking the firm steps topping the rise.
The hills then stood in spring-fresh beauty,
An expanding landscape met your eye.

      Now in the valley the mood seems sombre,
      Dark and purple Ben Vorlich is now.
      Watch that walker climbing upwards,
      Feet, legs, body meeting the rise.
      Imagination climbs that hillside,
      Some fifty years have now gone past,
      Purple and dark the autumn heather.
      The steps you take, down here, are shaky,
      A pack's too much for you to bear,
      The hand that grasped a rock with sureness,
      Is trembling now, and stiff, and sore.

Imagine now as you were then,
And let regret steal back no more.

Arthur Merrall

MEMORIES OF THE SIXTIES

Back in the sixties when we made love not war
we'd never had it so good,
but we wanted more, more, more,
if you wanted a night out with your honey
you just asked for extra pocket money.

No mugging then, just pot and mead,
warnings from "the Parents" we never did heed,
a generation not interested in power
would just as soon hand you a flower.

Colour TV was something new,
"boutiques" sold the clothes FOR YOU.
Dance halls let you round the back,
no-one cared if they got the sack.

The "Beatles" happened in Liverpool,
Followed by the Stones and Brian Poole.
Kaftans were the thing to wear,
they say if you remember it, you wasn't really there.

People had only just started going places –
Cilla Black and the Small Faces.
Pubs were strictly for the birds,
clubs were where all the sounds were heard.

Minis became very common,
and motor-bikes were no good for lovin' –
you couldn't do your courtin' on the back,
that's why everyone wanted a Ford Zodiac.

C.A. Coulson

A MASK 2

Out from behind fashion's frenzy,
         you'd glide down the catwalks of dreams.
Your mannequin mask never smiling:–
         "It's the garment that's meant to be seen."
Then stare into fashion-shoot camera,
         not a flicker betrays what's within:–
Are you real?   Are you warm?   Can you scream? –
Do you storm?
         Were you ever really that thin?

Then Cover-Girl, covered in furs, and diamonds
         flashing their lights,
Flash bulbs too, and then you need do
         frantic shopping for stockings and tights.
For tomorrows began with Hairdresser's hands,
         teasing with tongs and tattle:–
The Duchess of This,
         and the Countess of That,
         in endless, senseless prattle!
His final touch, pretty glitter dust,
         to set off a hat to perfection!

Thirty years on, you'd look back and laugh:–
         'til a touch from another direction.
A darkness had deigned.   They'd tried to explain,
         that Parkinson's was the connection.
His mask can be frozen expression,
         but never your eyes can dim,
By a God-given grace, yours is the face,
         love ensures,
         will be lit from within.

         Robert Bogue

SECOND TIME AROUND

The world has changed –
Become a wondrous place,
As I, like an excited child,
Behold your smiling face.

We are not young.
Not teenagers, out on a first date.
For both of us have reached
The noon-tide of our lives.

Yes, it was love at first sight,
That day on which we met.
Each strolling in the park.
Feeling lonely, getting wet.

Our eyes – his blue, mine hazel, met,
And lightning filled the air,
We smiled, we walked, we talked.
The atmosphere alive with tension.

Love hit us like a thunderbolt.
The world turned upside-down.
This second chance to love and care
Came at the speed of sound.

Joined to each other by this bond,
In sickness and in health,
We've found a depth of feeling,
An honest, trusting, lasting, loving wealth

OF HAPPINESS AND CONTENTMENT.

Betty Robertson

AN OLD MAN

Once I was young and agile,
With a mind full of hope and joy.
I thought that youth was endless,
As I lived my life as a boy.
Now I am old and wrinkled,
My body is stiff and bent.
And I sit and wonder where
Those precious years all went.

Lynda Moreby

DILLY DALLY DAYS

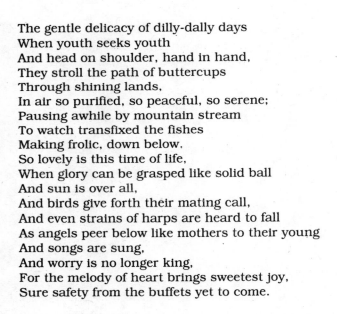

The gentle delicacy of dilly-dally days
When youth seeks youth
And head on shoulder, hand in hand,
They stroll the path of buttercups
Through shining lands,
In air so purified, so peaceful, so serene;
Pausing awhile by mountain stream
To watch transfixed the fishes
Making frolic, down below.
So lovely is this time of life,
When glory can be grasped like solid ball
And sun is over all,
And birds give forth their mating call,
And even strains of harps are heard to fall
As angels peer below like mothers to their young
And songs are sung,
And worry is no longer king,
For the melody of heart brings sweetest joy,
Sure safety from the buffets yet to come.

James Culwick

INVISIBLE BARRIERS

Walls stand between us – you and I.
Invisible to a stranger's eye,
We're caged apart until we die.

Barriers of words that stand unseen,
Double-glazed, chilled ice between,
Erected by comments we didn't mean.

Splintered words and clustered sound
Slamming hard onto frozen ground.
Wound as deep as the devil's hound.

Too late to wish such words unsaid;
Like Damocles' sword high overhead,
Love twists on a tooth-strings thread.

Regrets can never break walls down,
Like painted smiles on an unfrocked clown,
Apologies mask a tragic frown.

Walls of words must be torn apart,
Then rebuilt to make a new start –
Papering over a crack-crazed heart.

So small the tongue that split the words,
And smaller yet the ear which heard;
But wise the mind that knew them absurd.

Janis Priestley

41

ENGLAND REMEMBERED

I STILL remember England
When acorns filled the lanes,
Clear bubbling streams ran swift and pure,
Supplied by summer rains,
Small stickle-backs, glass jars and string
Were part of growing pains.

Through fields of green they wandered free,
Small urchin boys at play,
Their poverty a uniform
That dressed them every day,
Each one had hopes and futile dreams,
We all grew up that way.

Still I remember England
Before her roads grew wide,
When clean canals lazed in the sun,
Blackberries filled each side,
We saw the boats and swam along
Just hoping for a ride.

Children then were poorly clad
But equal in their plight,
As I recall our humble bed
Where six could sleep each night,
Yet none denies the memory
When happiness was right.

Yes I remember England,
The way it was before,
Though life was poor, each family nursed
A friendship at their door,
Until there came another call
And off she went to war.

So many times she trembled,
Yet every time she stood,
She held her ground, defied the threats,
Despite her guns of wood,
The oceans swilled to cleanse her wounds
To rid the shores of blood.

The wives remember England
When first they heard the foe,
Those women saw what they had feared –
Their menfolk had to go,
Young mothers faced the clouds alone
In shelters down below.

So dark and drear those early days,
With innocence abused,
Deep sadness spread across the land,
Made elderly confused,
In every house no waste was made
And every grain was used.

And they remember England,
The men who had to die,
Who faced the gust of savage war
And asked no questions why,
They took the pain so we could live
Beneath a safer sky.

And when it was all over,
Grand parties were our treat,
Hearts overflowed with passioned joy,
Much dancing filled the street,
Into the night the fires burned
As sleep came on our feet.

So I remember England,
No matter where I've been,
For she remains my favourite land
Despite the changes seen,
When I am gone, I pray to lie
As dust on England's green.

After the war

F. Ball

CHILDHOOD

My quest took me back
        to the streets of my childhood,
To humble beginnings
        where my living began,
And where my first learnings
        through years of my boyhood,
Prepared me for treading
        in the world as a man.

I stood there in wonder
        with old thoughts beguiling,
My mind drifted back
        to the games we knew then,
And the kids growing with me
        all ruddy but smiling,
Came back with my memories
        like ghosts of the men.

Though poor as we were
        in those times long ago,
We shared a contentment
        in poverty's wake,
Armed only with envy,
        few crimes we would know,
Excepting small mischiefs
        for devilment's sake.

So I watched them more,
        those kids who ran playing,
Their pitch was the roadway,
        each kerb stone a line,
And in their young voices,
        through words they were saying,
Came dreams and ambitions
        exactly like mine.

We chose our two teams
     for those games long ago,
Our ball was a tin can,
     the goalposts were trees,
The rules were our own make,
     so altered, but also
Young girls were our quarry
     to chase and to tease.

Long coarse baggy trousers
     patched roughly and torn,
Failed always to cover
     my red wounded knee,
Socks drooped at the ankles,
     shoes laceless and worn,
We treasured the value
     of good company.

Just willing to play
     from dawn's early light,
Chalked wickets were marked
     on walls, gates or poles.
We played until sunset,
     saw day turn to twilight,
Lost count of the hours
     but shared all the goals.

Our trait was to fill
     each pocket with treasure,
Blunt penknives and marbles,
     catapults and things,
Small value indeed
     except for the pleasure
Of saving old milk tops
     or top and whip strings.

When rain filled the gutters,
     swift rivers flowed free,
Our boats were used matches
     discarded as waste,
But we raced each other
     like ships on the sea,
Young pride was the power,
     enjoyment the haste.

When winter came calling,
     long slide rakes were laid,
We slid the hard surface
     despite adult cries,
Snowflakes were most welcome
     as snowmen were made,
Each face smiling coldly
     with coal chips for eyes.

We stayed until darkness,
     gas lamps lit our way,
Just poor shabby kids
     in the cool evening air,
Doors closing in taverns
     closed also our day,
With love on street corners
     Abandoned right there.

But back today
     with my errand completed,
I still hear the voices
     'though silent and gone,
The streets have matured
     as time is defeated,
Our era has faded
     but memories live on.

F. Ball

DARK IS KIND

I
like
the dark.
The craggy
lines of age
are blurred
then gone.
And I
can believe
I have, once more,
my slender girlish form

And dream again
of dancing till dawn broke,
with all those young men
who pledged their love,
only to learn
I was not for them.

Or think, perhaps
of weddings. Of my own
to my best beloved.
Now, too old to mourn,
his death has left me
once again, alone.

Could I return
to the springtime of my youth?
I would not think it right.
How rich my life has been.
I valued it;
but now – the dark is kind.

Janis Priestley

ONCE IN A LIFETIME

Today I walk amongst the trees, there was a beech,
Through the park where children played. I was alone.
Today I walked amongst the crowd and tried to reach,
Perhaps too much, I'll never know. I was alone.

The sun had risen, the dew was gold,
My gold was with me. I was alone.
I looked and felt and thought it bold,
And yet despite it all, I was still alone.

Another time amongst the trees there was a dream,
Through the park where children played, far from home.
It was a time of two as one, beside the stream,
I was with you and not alone.

Alone is just a state of being, I have a dream,
Not my words, I know, another man's alone.
Stand beside me, beside that stream,
To give you love and life, no more alone.

Your love alone gives such joy, a play on words?
A play perhaps that has no end, I have a dream.
My dream is yours, have you not heard,
Love, like life, has no start nor end, it's like a stream.

Edward Urry

THE PATCH

It's only a patch
Just round the back
To reap and then savour
The fruits of your labour
You can't do better than that.

You can do what you will
With the herbs on the sill
The lettuce competes
Alongside the beet
You can't do better than that.

In the growbags aligned
Tomatoes you'll find
Even the barrow
Harvests a marrow
You can't do better than that.

The lawn looks a treat
There's even a seat
On the trellis around
The clematis abounds
You can't do better than that.

The baskets are ablaze
With colours that amaze
The alpines delight
On the site that's just right
You can't do better than that.

To the birds and the bees
It's a haven indeed
Abolish the sprays
That pollute the airways
You can't do better than that.

When your limbs start to ache
And you feel like a break
Just sit and savour
The fruits of your labour
What could be nicer than that?

Hazel Cuthbertson

Feelings

Why did I not shout,
And jump for joy
At what I could do –
No problem?

MY LOVE

Love for to hold you,
Love to caress,
Bless you for being the whole world to me.
See you all smart, a glistening sight,
Hair so golden and eyes that delight and brighten my love.
My joy of the morning,
The peace of the evening,
Song of my heart, enraptured expressing
Purest of love and loveliest notions,
Delicate hands and sweetest of potions
To perfume and heighten my delicate senses
And drive me like madness
Back home to my homestead
To free you from sadness
And hold you so tight,
So tight in the night, my love.

James Culwick

MY LOVE DIED

I used to love a little when I was young and tender
But love was thrown into my teeth
        and hated by the sender.
Gone many years
        and now I have the chance to love once more;
But so much fear is mixed in it that it can never pour,
Freely and beautifully as it did,
It merely trickles underneath the lid.

                    James Culwick

HOLIDAY POSTCARDS
or
BE STILL MY TREMBLING HAND

I'm sending you this postcard just to say
This holiday was really quite unplanned;
Weather was fine, so we just came away.
Be still my trembling hand.

We're staying at this cottage on the cliff,
With lovely views across to Ireland.
Had lots of walks, my legs are getting stiff,
But not my trembling hand.

Been swimming in the lovely warm blue sea,
Sunbathing after on the golden sand.
Caught many shrimps, but then I set them free
With my own trembling hand.

Walked out along the ancient wooden pier,
And listened to the local village band.
They played music which we love to hear,
Be still my trembling hand.

My writing on this card is getting small,
I hope that you can read and understand.
Parkinson's Disease has made my scrawl
Exacerbate my shaking, trembling hand.

Hey, what is happening up there in the sky?
Sea mists are rolling in across the land.
Time to go in; So I must write Goodbye,
With my own trembling hand.

Tim Clarke

APOLOGIES

If you think that I am shaking
With stage-fright: don't worry please.
'Tis not fear that causes quaking,
I've got Parkinson's Disease.

Just because I stand here trembling,
Don't look really at my ease.
I have difficulty remembering,
'Cos of Parkinson's Disease.

If a bus I may be taking,
And by chance, against you squeeze.
Does the engine cause the shaking,
Or my Parkinson's Disease?

If at meal times I am rocking,
Cannot hold a spoon of peas,
Or against the plate am knocking,
That is Parkinson's Disease.

Or, perhaps you see me drinking,
Spilling beer down on my knees.
I'm not drunk as you are thinking,
Just blame Parkinson's Disease.

Or when walking I am stumbling,
Or my footsteps start to freeze.
Even out of bed come tumbling
Down with Parkinson's Disease.

If you think that I am grumbling
At my plight; forgive me please.
It is very, very humbling
Having Parkinson's Disease.

                              Tim Clarke

If, the poem below, was contributed by Dorothy Parker and was recited to her in Capetown, South Africa.

IF

Just a line to say I'm living,
That I'm not among the dead,
Though I'm getting more forgetful,
And mixed up in the head.

I've got used to my arthritis,
To my dentures I'm resigned,
I can manage my bifocals,
But, my word, I miss my mind.

Sometimes I can't remember
When I'm standing by the stair,
If I should go up for something
Or if I've just come down from there.

And before the fridge so often,
My mind is filled with doubt.
Now, did I put some food away
Or come to take it out?

If it's not my turn to write, dear,
I hope you won't get sore.
I may think that I have written
And don't want to be a bore.

So remember I do love you
And wish that you lived near.
And now it's time to mail this
And to say goodbye, my dear.

Now I stand before the pillar box
And my face is very red –
Instead of posting this to you,
I opened it instead.

Anonymous

56

MY BRIGHT RED TIGHTS

Oh! How I wish I did not shake
And feel so sorry for myself
I want to scream
I want to swear
To tell the world... It's damned unfair!

But as I get up from my bed
And plan what I will wear
I rummage through my undies drawer
Cursing pity and despair
I spot the very thing I need
To cheer and raise my sights
Today I'll be defiant... In my lovely bright red tights!

When in a bloody-minded mood
Well then... I will rebel
I'll tell the world to 'Go to hell'
I'll curse this thing
I know my rights... I'll wear my bright red tights!

You may not like the words I use
So we must disagree
For the odd expletive keeps me sane
Against this thing which hinders me
This curse we call PD.

So when in a defiant mood
To stop me feeling BLUE
I rummage in my undies drawer
Full of thermal wool delights
What bucks me up? What makes me smile?
Oh my lovely BRIGHT RED TIGHTS.

                              Vina Curren

THE HOUSE ON THE HILL NEAR GOLDEN BAY

The air is filled with excitement
A hush settles now everyone's in
Musicians appear to loud applause
And the minstrel's tunes begin
The dancers dance to wild violins,
To mandolins and Spanish guitars
The drums beat out a rhythm
Beneath the moon and stars
And the music flows in a magical way
At the house on the hill near Golden Bay.

Michaelangelo and Rembrandt
Have paintings in each corner and niche
There's beauty everywhere you look
Each room a masterpiece
The walls and ceilings overflow
With creations by the Old Masters
Renoir, Cezanne and Degas
Are stretched from floor to rafters
You can see them when you spend a day
At the house on the hill near Golden Bay.

There are deer herds roaming in the fields
Peacocks and pheasant walk around
A forest forms the backdrop
Behind that snowcapped peaks abound
Swans gracefully glide the rivers
Where trout and salmon leap
An idyllic vision before your eyes
A memory to savour and keep
Where down in the sea the dolphins play
Before the house on the hill near Golden Bay.

The cinema shows movies by the great
     directors of screen
And the photographic collection is the
     best ever seen
The sporting facilities are second to none
The hall of fame has a display of every
     sports Number One
The library is filled with masterworks
     of fiction and fact
There are walls of encyclopedias and
     reference books racked:
All the knowledge you'd ever need, and
     without doubt the best.
Or if you preferred to, you can just lay
     there and rest
By the pool in the sun, that shines
     every day
At the house on the hill near Golden Bay.

Gordon Martin

PARKINSON'S DISEASE

Once, when I moved,
My body moved too.
It knew what to do.
No problem.

Once, when I walked,
My legs walked too.
They knew what to do.
No problem.

Once, when I turned,
My feet turned too.
They knew what to do.
No problem.

Once, when I hurried,
My limbs hurried too.
They knew what to do.
No problem.

Once, when I worked,
My hands worked too.
They knew what to do.
No problem.

Once, when I wrote,
My hand wrote too.
It knew what to do.
No problem.

Once, when I spoke,
My voice spoke too.
It knew what to do.
No problem.

Once, when I smiled,
My face smiled too.
It knew what to do.
No problem.

So why did I not smile,
Smile all the time,
To have such skills –
No problem?

Why did I not shout,
And jump for joy
At what I could do –
No problem?

But I didn't know
These things could go,
Just disappear,
No problem.

Now I remember the time
When my body was free,
Its movements were mine.
No problem.

The hardest to tolerate
Is not hands or feet,
But the unthinking ways
Of some people I meet.

I walk very strangely,
And dribble my drink,
Drop my food like a toddler
So what should they think?

They look and assume
– In their eyes I can tell –
That if I do these things,
Then I'm stupid as well.
No problem!

M.R. Henley

61

PRAYERS

If all of my prayers could be answered,
What a wonderful world it would be,
No pain, and no suffering, no worries or fears,
The animals, all happy and free.

If all of my prayers could be answered,
They all must be honest and true,
Sincere, and unselfish, undemanding and loving,
Embracing this world, and the Spirit world too.

If all of my prayers could be answered,
I wonder how good it would feel
To know that the people I'd prayed for and hoped for
Were suddenly granted their will.

If all of my prayers could be answered,
Would the world become better and new?
Would the love and the friendship and peace
                              spread all over,
Or only reach out to the few?

If all of my prayers could be answered,
What a wonderful world it would be
Just to suddenly find, every person was kind,
Including us all, you and me.

If all of us tried a bit harder
To know one another and live
A life that was full of just nothing but love
And a longing to constantly give.

Together we all could work wonders,
United, and linked just as one,
Our faith could make miracles happen around us
And everything good would be done.

But if all of my prayers could be answered,
Would it only be me that was pleased?
Would the things that I pray for,
                          be things I am wishing,
Just letting my conscience be eased?

But I ask if my prayers can be answered
Only if God thinks it's right,
For whatever He does is the best for our souls,
He will show us the pathway to light.

If all of my prayers could be answered,
Whatever I humbly should say,
It will be for the best, and the good, and the right,
Knowing the answers will all be God's way.

                          Doris E. Taylor

Kate, the writer of this poem, was unable to speak, but was occasionally seen to write. After her death, in a geriatric hospital, her locker was emptied and this poem was found.

CRABBIT OLD WOMAN

What do you see, nurses,
        what do you see?
Are you thinking when
        you're looking at me
A crabbit old woman
        not very wise,
Uncertain of habit
        with far-away eyes,
Who dribbles her food
        and makes no reply
When you say in a loud voice
        "I do wish you'd try",
Who seems not to notice
        the things that you do,
And forever is losing
        a stocking or shoe,
Who unresisting or not
        lets you do as you will
With bathing and feeding,
        the long day to fill,
Is that what you're thinking,
        is that what you see?

Then open your eyes, nurse,
        you're not looking at me.
I'll tell you who I am
        as I sit here so still,
As I use at your bidding,
        as I eat at your will.

64

I'm a small child of ten
      with a father and mother,
Brothers and sisters
      who love one another,
A young girl of sixteen
      with wings on her feet,
Dreaming that soon now
      a lover she'll meet:
A bride soon at twenty,
      my heart gives a leap,
Remembering the vows
      that I promised to keep:
At twenty-five now
      I have young of my own
Who need me to build
      a secure happy home.
A young woman of thirty,
      my young now grow fast,
Bound to each other
      with ties that should last:
At forty my young ones
      now grown will soon be gone,
But my man stays beside me
      to see I don't mourn:
At fifty once more
      babies play round my knee,
Again we know children,
      my loved one and me.
Dark days are upon me,
      my husband is dead,
I look at the future,
      I shudder with dread,
For my young are all busy
      rearing young of their own,
And I think of the years
      and the love I have known.

I'm an old woman now
     and nature is cruel,
'Tis her jest to make
     old age look like a fool.
The body it crumbles,
     grace and vigour depart,
There now is a stone
     where once I had a heart:
But inside this old carcass
     a young girl still dwells,
And now and again
     my battered heart swells,
I remember the joys,
     I remember the pain,
And I'm loving and living
     life over again,
I think of the years
     all too few – gone too fast,
And accept the stark fact
     that nothing can last
So open your eyes, nurses,
     open and see,
Not a crabbit old woman,
     look closer – see ME.

Kate

A POEM IS A BEAUTIFUL GIFT

I have no roses to leave for you
From the wilderness of my trust,
To waft sweet fragrances heav'nward
Carrying echoes of my love.

I bear no honeyed sweetmeats
As I scale your garden wall,
Nor perfumed lace to hand you
Wrapped in bows and gilded foil.

Nor polished autumn apples
Laid in whisp'ring purple nests,
Shining with golden goodness
To tempt your hand's caress.

But the gift that I would bring to you
Is an expression of my love.
A poem I would sing for you
In the still of the twilight hush.

                              Janis Priestley

LIFE

Life is for laughing,
For genuine mirth,
For spreading true kindness
And treasuring birth.

Life is for giving,
Dividing the spoil,
For mixing the workload,
Then sharing the toil.

Life is a present,
A gift from on high,
No brother should change it,
Not you, and not I.

Life is for planting
The trees of fond care,
Yet also to poison
The seeds of despair.

Life's cup fills with pride,
With strong noble thought,
Respect is the trophy
That cannot be bought.

Life is for showing
The best you can give,
Ensuring true solace,
Where others may live.

Life is for loving,
For harbouring truth,
And cooling the young heat
From impetuous youth.

Life is a weapon,
To wield and destroy,
The greed of a grown man,
The spite of the boy.

Life is a contest
When trouble prevails,
Love is the hurdle
Where avarice fails.

Life is a pleasure
If selflessly meant,
Then life is for laughing
When honestly spent.

F. Ball

THEY CERTAINLY WEREN'T THINGS...

They certainly weren't things that the average person would
associate with anything serious. A bit of an achey feeling in
my leg when driving. Shakiness in my arm and hand.
Illegible and slow handwriting.

Doing crafts, my love and at that time my livelihood,
became more and more difficult. I acquired an awkward and
stiff gait. Somehow the message didn't seem to be
getting through to my various body parts. Something was
applying the brakes to *Miss One-Hundred-and-One-Miles-an-
Hour*.

Stress. Yes, that was it. Retail and Christmas, plus a
slumping economy, two pre-teens and the single life. All
good reasons to be stressed out. There just wasn't time to
see a doctor, and besides, anyone as generally healthy as
me would get over this in time. A good rest perhaps, a week
away and everything would be fine again.

Unfortunately, the holiday came and went and the
symptoms persisted. Finally persuaded to see a doctor, I
did. Brainscans, an M.R.I. and 'Evoked Potential Testing' at
McMaster failed to show any abnormalities. My doctor said
that he suspected Parkinson's disease.

Other than general observations by the doctor, there
really isn't any way to conclusively diagnose this illness
other than by eliminating everything else. The best way
to decide if this was indeed the correct diagnosis was to pre-
scribe the accepted medication, and if it worked then *voila!*
– diagnosis made. The medication did indeed work, and
the pronouncement was made. Parkinson's.

Parkinson's? But I was only 35 years old! That's a
disease that only happens to 'old' people. And other
people. Not me! Off to the library to research this topic
where I found three books about Parkinson's. All showed
pictures of stooped, white haired people in advanced stages
of the illness. Advice was given on how to stop from falling,
how to avoid drooling, how to get up out of a chair. Nothing
I read said anything about how to cope at my age. What

about my daily life, employment, my children, my parents, *my future*!

My reaction was to hide the disease for as long as possible. I continued on as best I could and, with the medication that was prescribed, I was feeling not too badly. The symptoms could be controlled quite well, and except for nausea and dizziness caused by one of the medications, I felt OK. I tried to continue doing everything I had done before, basically trying to ignore what was happening.

Only my close friends knew about it and it wasn't something I really wanted to broadcast. Why? Maybe I didn't want to be different, or think that anyone might pity me. Maybe I was denying it myself, and if I didn't verbalize it, it would go away or at least recede to where I didn't have to deal with it.

To be told that I have a degenerative, neurological disease, that it can only get worse no matter what I do, to know that the pictures in the Parkinson's handbook of old people is what I will be like eventually (barring any miracle drugs or discoveries) is not fun. To know that I will require assistance one day with every activity I now take for granted is humbling. With the help of drugs, the first years of this disease can physically pass fairly smoothly. The general public is probably not generally aware of it and that could make it seem that there really isn't a problem. The seeming normalness on the outside does not show the trauma that needs to be dealt with inside.

Everyone is different and handles their problems their own way. The only way I know to handle things is to be optimistic. Some may say this is not realistic. Some may call me a Pollyanna. Others may think that this disease is obviously a piece of cake, so what's the big deal? Just because I'm not letting it get me down doesn't mean it doesn't scare me. It does. It frustrates me and makes me angry. Frustrates me because my abilities are limited. Angers me because I have to ask 'why me?' and there is no answer.

Five very eventful years have passed since I was diagnosed. I have since sold my store, and worked for an accounting office. I had to give that job up in February as it proved to be too much to handle. While working in the accountant's office, I learned that computers can be very friendly. Now, instead of reaching people and making them smile through my crafts, I can hopefully touch them through the written word. I have gone through the different stages, from denial to acceptance to a zeal to share my experiences. I want people to know the symptoms of this disease, to seek early medical help and to not be afraid to let other people know. More and more young people are developing Parkinson's disease and awareness of symptoms is so important.

From the other side of the fence, I want people to have a little more patience. Be a little more considerate when I'm slow at the grocery checkout, don't look at me as if I've had too much to drink when I stumble, and please try to be patient when I have trouble writing out a cheque.

I can honestly say that the past few years have been the best of my life. New doors are opening all over for me and I am constantly stretching my comfort zone. Experiences I never would have dreamed of having present themselves almost daily and opportunities to help others are popping up all over. I want people to appreciate the little things. I want them to see the humour in day to day life that all too often is missed because we are in too much of a hurry.

Of course Parkinson's disease is not pleasant. The current prognosis is not encouraging, although research is ongoing. Just as I'm becoming more confident, and self-assured, more aware and more adventurous, my body is becoming excruciatingly slow. I don't enjoy having to ask someone to cut my meat.

I don't enjoy the problems I often have walking, the fatigue, the depression or the involuntary movements caused by this illness. Who would? But it has taught me tolerance, to reassess my priorities, and that, yes, things could be a whole lot worse.

Lynda McKenzie

IS THERE SOMETHING WRONG?

I hate it when those people stare
While I am sitting on my chair.
I came here for a pleasant meal,
But furtive looks they seem to steal.

It isn't nice while seated there,
Aware that all those people stare
As I chase peas around my plate –
My heart beats fast at such a rate.

I wish that they could understand,
The way I shake – it's just not planned.
My face is turning beetroot red –
Was it something that I said?

I wish that I could hide my face
In some distant, far-off place,
And calm myself, be placid, still –
With peace and quiet get my fill.

I just wish people understood
The problem we have with our food –
When from my chair I start to rise,
I hardly dare lift up my eyes.

But I'll be brave and stand up straight,
With all my might I'll concentrate,
And stand up tall, hold my head high,
I'll look those folk straight in the eye.

It's not my fault I have a shake,
I really CAN'T put on the brake.
But I WILL hold my head up high,
AND look them ALL straight in the eye!

Margaret Hooper

73

WISHING

I wish I didn't have to mumble,
I wish I didn't have to fumble
              or tumble
BUT I DO

I wish I could remember names,
I wish that I could still play games
BUT I CAN'T

I'd love to make a chocolate cake
BUT I CAN'T
I wish I didn't always shake
BUT I DO

I wish I didn't hesitate
To remember every date
BUT I DO

I wish my tremble didn't show,
I wish I didn't walk so slow
BUT IT DOES – AND I DO

I wish that I could write a letter
BUT I CAN'T

HOW I wish I could get better!
BUT I WON'T.

BE BRAVE.

                    Margaret Hooper

PARKINSONISM

I used to go walking with you over mountains,
and strolling together 'long rocky sea shore.
But Parkinsonism restricts easy movements,
and even a short walk is like a great chore.

I used to climb tall poies to mend telephone wires,
and gallop on horse-back down wild country lanes.
But Parkinsonism means I no more can do that,
for even a short trot brings on many pains.

I used to draw blue-prints to exacting details,
and fill in the figures with fine mapping pen.
But Parkinsonism so gets my hand shaking,
that my writing resembles the tracks of a hen.

Now scientists have found that monkeys affected
with Parkinsonism can have brain repair.
How the poor creatures got it defies contemplation,
but it means that we humans need never despair.

So let's pray, my darling, that in the near future,
Parkinsonism becomes a disease of the past.
So that once again its many poor sufferers
can walk and relax and stop shaking at last.

Tim Clarke

SO MUCH LOVE

So much love
A tiny child can bring
To the face of man or king.
The new child cherished within your arms
Evokes such tenderness
No-one will harm
This tiny child.

So much love,
The pain has gone,
I hold him close
And look upon
His tiny face
And proudly see
This child whose place
Is here with me.

So much love
Surrounds this child,
I look at him,
Then look at you.
This child is here
Because we two
Could share our love,
A family now.

So much love
This child creates,
Proud grandparents
Fondly wait
Their chance to hold this child,
This special tiny child.
So much love.

Peggy (Gran) Lowndes
To David Thomas Lowndes

EARLY ONE MORNING

I've been up and down
And wobbled around
For most of the night till dawn.
Watched satellite TV,
Brewed endless pots of tea,
With never so much as a yawn.

I fought with the shower
At an ungodly hour,
Shampooed my hair, and the ceiling!
With toothbrush I battled
As my poor teeth it rattled
While clinging to sink, soap and flannel.

Collapsed on a stool,
And I felt such a fool
As I sneezed, really shaking the house,
Then with strong rubber glove,
Thanking heaven above,
My glasses, retrieved from the loo!

When disinfected and dried,
With them I espied
A massive black spider above me.
He got me quite riled,
Just dangled - and smiled,
Then fell with a plop, in my tea!

I got dressed in my clothes,
When I'd straightened my toes
And got limbs to respond to my brain.
There on the bed
My clothes were all spread,
Suddenly I'm off, like a train!

"Hang on! my jumper,"
It was on back to front
And the zip on my skirt caught my nose!
One shoe I had found
No trouble at all –
Where's the other one? God only knows!

Can't cope with stockings
So I've moved on to tights,
As suspenders I got in a knot,
Then perched on the bed,
My knees to my head,
I laddered both legs – the lot!

I've had to wear socks,
With a pattern like rocks
And the cardigan knitted by Mum,
With the extra large buttons,
So easy to fasten,
Unless you have my fat tum!

I've now found my shoe,
Well I had, till it flew!
Can't give up, as I'm almost there.
I sit by the mirror
With body aquiver,
Now fingers refuse to comb hair!

RIGHT! THAT'S IT, THAT'S ENOUGH,
I'm all out of puff,
'Switched off' and it's only just nine!
Well who's here to know
If I stop, start or go?
So I'll relax, and just take my time.

                              Rosemary Jones

REMEMBER I'M STILL ME

I know I'm growing shaky
My tremors I can't hide
But please remember when we meet
That I'm still ME inside.

My words may not come easily
For you to understand
But can't you see I really want
To smile and shake your hand.

Don't leave me in a corner
Forgetting that I'm there
I'm part of life the same as you
And need your loving care.

Fate has dealt this sorry blow
It cannot be denied
But remember when you look at me
That I'm still ME inside.

Margaret Randall

THE GUITAR

When I hear my son a' strumming
On his guitar, I join him humming,
Sometimes I wonder if the plumbing
Is going to join in with the drumming.

His shelves will all be piling up
With some monstrous Silver Cup,
We will have to keep them clean
And I'll set on my Mr. Sheen!

So my courage I will muster
And I'll try hard not to fluster
As I wield my hateful duster,
They MUST HAVE a shiny lustre
SAFE AND SOUND FROM ANY RUST-er!

                    Margaret Hooper

LET IT BE

With hindsight now, I see it all –
The stumbling step, the silly fall,
Days of tiredness, spirits flagging,
Walks with one foot somehow dragging.
Deep inside a nagging dread,
Ominous snatches of things read.

Well-meant concern from caring folk
Rebuffed, repelled – "it's all a joke –
It's just my age, no I'm alright."
I do not wish to share my plight.

The palsied shake of wilful hands –
"Please let me cope with life's demands."
These silent prayers pour from my heart,
Of Parkinson's I want no part.
I *know* tomorrow I'll be fine –
My hands are stilled, a certain sign.

With hindsight now I see so well
I lived in self-inflicted hell.
How difficult I made each day,
Just wishing *it* would go away.

My husband's plea to share my life,
To be allowed to help his wife,
Mother, sister, friends all tried,
"I don't need pity," I replied,
Stubborn, cross, devoid of humour,
Anger spreading like a tumour.

With hindsight now I see it all,
From stumbling step to silly fall,
Love surrounds me, people care,
Now at last I learn to share!

Diane Rule

81

THE FLOWER

If you look at a flower in the morning,
And it's closed up as tight as can be,
Do you wonder about its beauty,
Do you wonder, what you will see
When the sun begins to warm it,
And its face begins to show,
Do you wonder about the flower,
Do you compare it with someone you know?

I think of that flower in the morning
And compare it with my life, you see
I'm very similar to the flower,
I can close up as tight as can be,
It's because this disease known as Parkinson's
Makes me sometimes not able to show
My face, like the flower in the garden,
My expression's closed up, this I know.

But if, as I hope, in the daytime,
My beauty shows through, I won't mind,
When the night time comes, like the flower,
And once again, a closed up person you'll find.
Because I know very soon, if I'm lucky,
This flower, which is just like me,
Will bloom, morning, noon and night time,
For all the world to see.

Hilary Claydon

THE NEW POET

One winter's day when I felt rough,
And life to me seemed very tough,
I saw my YAPMAG lying there,
I swooped it up and took a chair.

When I was settled down to read,
I soon found news to fill my need.
One little piece said 'Can you write,'
My words flowed quickly into sight.

So pen to paper I did put,
My mind to everything was shut.
Life for me swept quickly by
I didn't even need to cry!

I forgot that I was feeling blue,
I hope you'll find a talent too.
It's wonderful to know that you
May some day be a poet too.

So here's to you and here's to me,
When you jot down all that you see
And by the fire one winter's night,
Take up your pen and start to write.

Margaret Hooper

ME AND MY PARKINSON'S

Me and My Parkinson's! Or you could say *Me and My Shadow*, because it's always with me, everywhere I go, wherever I am. We first became acquainted, my Parkinson's and I, just before my fortieth birthday, and I must say it came as quite a shock, as I'd been led to believe that *life* began at 40, not *Parkinson's*. However, I feel that I have accepted the situation now and am coming to terms with its vagaries. "You can get used to 'owt bar tight shoes," as my father used to say. As I recall, my father always did have a literary turn of phrase! He died when I was only young, but I still remember many of his odd sayings. I mean, could anywhere really be "as dark as a bowler hat with pockets in!"

However, I digress. Back to the matter in hand. Me and My Parkinson's! It's not at all like *Me and My Dog*! At least you can let someone else take the dog for a walk. Not so with Parkinson's. Parkinson's takes *you* for a walk, or not, depending on how the legs are affected that day.

It is my legs that seem to be most affected. Most of the time they feel tired or heavy or just about to collapse. Sometimes they tremble although the Sinemet tablets do usually eliminate the tremor. *Why should this be*? I ask myself. My legs always seemed ordinary enough, although I couldn't stop a pig in an entry, I must admit. To those uninitiated into the world of Derbyshire slang, this means that I'm bow-legged. Only slightly, mind you. As I once said to my husband when he commented on this slight flaw in my anatomy, "It's probably caused by carrying you about all these years!"

Someone very aptly described the way my legs often feel, as if I'm trying to walk in treacle! It can be very frustrating and I find that when my legs feel tired, so does the rest of me.

Me and My Parkinson's, maybe that should read *Me and My Scapegoat*! Because, rightly or wrongly, it takes the blame for all my failings. When I carry the tea tray into the lounge, merrily slopping tea as I go and liberally filling all the saucers, it's my Parkinson's that's making the mess, not me.

It's the same when I stumble over the slumbering dog stretched out on the hearth rug, causing yelps of anguish from the poor animal; my Parkinson's is to blame because I'm unsteady on my feet. "Let sleeping dogs lie!" Not a chance when I'm around!

I'm not limited to just inflicting grievous bodily harm on the canine of the family. I can even walk over my children's feet and be unable to alter course once my foot has started on its inexorable downward path. As my offspring invariably walk about the house without shoes, the resulting yells of pain and indignation can be heard right down the street.

Me and My Parkinson's! I think the emphasis should clearly be on the word "my" because my Parkinson's is in fact exclusive to me. Whilst having many of the same characteristics as yours, it is nevertheless very individual in its manifestation. And so I have to deal with it in my own way, as what works for you may not necessarily work for me. However, I do feel that we can all benefit from pooling our knowledge and airing our experiences and, who knows, we may yet push the gaunt spectre of Parkinson's disease further into the shadows.

Anne S. Limb

IF ONLY I

If I could spend my every hour
Watching grasses grow,
And see the sun tint every flower
What better could I know?

If I could hear a bluebell ring
With tunes decreed by me,
Then every bird would gladly sing
Sweet envy with the bee.

If I could melt the drifts of snow
That every year are seen,
Then frost and ice would quickly go
To leave dear England green.

If many words when joined by me
Could paint a sky at night,
Then every line would surely be
Worth time and space to write.

If people's dreams were mine to mould
Designs my very own,
My wish would turn their grief to gold,
With evil quite unknown.

And if these things could all come true
Tomorrow I would say,
Let every sky be summer blue
And spring be every day.

F. Ball

PAUSE TO PONDER

Have you given this a thought?
Then perhaps I think you ought,
Has it ever occurred to you
That a Parkinson has a high IQ?
And if I may be so bold,
Suggest they are of a genius mould.

Whatever path in life they chose,
Be it stage or poetry and prose,
Lecturers and the Captains of Trade,
Whichever choice of profession made,
Even, if in the ring they fought,
To be the best is what they sought.

Not content with a quiet mind,
Parkinson's are an obsessive kind,
In striving for perfection in life,
Did we set the brain in strife?

And so, in reaching to be the best,
We've ended up worse than the rest!

Jennie Kendall

INSOMNIA

I used to love to go to bed
And on the pillow rest my head,
While away an hour with a paperback story,
Then lie with Morpheus 'til the morning's glory.
But now I lie awake with pain,
Please will the drugs give me peace again?
My neck, my shoulder, my ankle, my hip,
I try to be brave but I've a trembling lip.
My husband sleeps, then a little snore –
Shall I wake him? I'm not sure.
I feel like a babe that has yet to learn
I can't sit up or toss or turn.
I say to my mate, "a strong arm please",
He knows if I move my pain will ease,
So in his sleep provides an arm secure,
Then I can try to dream once more.

What about my comfort? Let me give that a thought.
Pillows I've tried, even pure down he has bought.
I'd like to lie upon nothing, with nothing to touch,
Or am I asking for just a little too much.
Please, does anyone know a man?
You know, the one on the telly, the man who can.
The illusionist, the one who can levitate,
Send him tomorrow around about eight.
I'll give him my trust, my mind and my body.
And in this perfect scheme,
I'll float, I'll sleep, perchance to dream.

Jennie Kendall

88

BECAUSE YOU CARE

On the day we met, you said you would care,
A life full of love together we'd share.
And through the years this promise you kept,
You still tell me you care, though together we wept,
When we heard the news, what was wrong with me,
The specialist said that I have Pd.

But now those words have a different sound,
To care now means also being around.
To pick up the pieces and hold my hand,
When my spirits are low you understand.

You help me with my socks and shoes,
You find my pills which I seem to lose.
Just you being there helps me to cope,
When I look to the future and see no hope
Of that needed cure,
That my former self, to us, could restore.

So come my love and hold me tight,
We'll dream together through the night.
We'll dream this never happened to me,
I won't have, never have had,
This wretched Pd.

                    Jennie Kendall

ODE TO A POSTER

What is this mask? this effigy?
Is this what you see, when you look at me?

Those eyes that have a desperate stare
say "Abandon Hope, Ye who enter there,"
Is this what you see, when you look at me?

Imprisoned by lack of mobility,
imprisoned, entombed by my own body.
Is this what you see, when you look at me?

Let me tell you what I see,
when I look in the mirror,
and see an image of me.

I see eyes that smile,
though the face may be still.
A body that moves,
though not at my will.

A mind that thinks with clarity
and plans the day ahead for me.
I see a face that likes to feel the sun
as I think of the garden jobs to be done.

And if at the end of the day
my chosen tasks are not complete,
I've still won, I've overcome
this disability, that you seem to see,
when you look at me.

I don't need to hurry, I've time to chat,
No worries now of tax and vat,
I'm content with the sun, the flowers and bees,
the summer breeze that rustles the trees.

And I know when the time comes,
to leave fellow man,
I will have figured somehow
in God's earthly plan.

So, next time you have the audacity,
to draw what you think is a spectre of me,
just draw my tears, because you see
I'm not as brave as I pretend to be.

Jennie Kendall

TO FIND A CURE

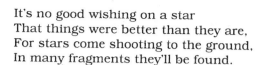

It's no good wishing on a star
That things were better than they are,
For stars come shooting to the ground,
In many fragments they'll be found.

Our lives, I think, must be like that –
Some lives, they just go pitter-pat,
But our lifestyle is so slow,
Things will not alter, that we know.

It's no good wishing for the moon,
or stars at night that twinkle soon,
But how we wish that we could say
'A cure will soon be on its way'.

As surely as the rain will pour,
Disease will stop at someone's door;
We wish we could change everything,
For if we could, the world would sing.

Illness should not creep around,
Confronting us without a sound.
If only we could truly say
That our disease had gone away.

If it did, the sun would shine –
Every day would be just fine.
The man up in the moon would laugh,
His beam would make a silvery path.

A myriad stars would wink above,
(Surely signs of our Lord's love),
Nature WILL NOT have its way –
We'll find a cure for us some day!

We'll work so hard in every way,
We WILL NOT have those feet of clay.
We're going to prove that we can fight,
Then everything will turn out right!

Margaret Hooper

91

FROMLOADING

Downloading a message or a file
Has nothing to do with feeling "Down",
It is a matter of saying, it is so called computerstyle.

Back to the sixties when computers became a common part,
The Beatles already sang about feeling
                              "Down, Down to the ground",
Is it since, that I'm feeling down sometimes, was it the start?

Did I load myself down, down to the ground of Mother Earth?
No I did not! It just started and after twenty years I found
Once should not load *Down* but *Up*, because life it's worth.

Uploading is like giving things with your heart,
                              like friendship and love.
Although it is often not accepted without any scepsis
                              or even with a rejecting sound
Of silence, everybody should hear about people loading *up*:
                    That's enough.

No Downloading in my dictionary, the word is badly chosen,
Just loading *From* and *To*,
                    Nobody should be singing around about "down",
Because "from" is much more friendly spoken.

So this message should reach every modem-user
                              in this world –
From now on we are *From-* and *To-loading*
                              because it is a better sound;
The sound of those who are often down,
                              but rather speak of "off".

                                        Kees Paap

THE IMPOSTER

Who is that person living in my body?
Why does he take over the steering
   whenever he likes?

Hey, you, inside me, stay off the brakes,
Let me take some pills,
   then I can kick you out of my life.

But he is very strong, this imposter,
He is not leaving
   although I'm dancing the jive.

Wilder and wilder, and he is still not leaving.
I take some more pills,
Then I KICK you out of my life!!!

Good, he's taking a rest so I can talk to this guy
And ask him: "will you please get out of my life?"

He won't listen to begging or threatening,
   so we now share this body,
We argued a lot but finally laid down the knife.

We are working together now
   in this 44 year old body.
I'm working, working and working,
   that's because I like.

There is so much to be done, I do it WITH him
Every day is the start, of the rest of my life.

                                        Kees Paap

93

BEHIND THE MASK

Behind the mask you see
The person that is me.

My body is so sick,
My brain reacts so quick.

My life's become so slow,
I was so fast, although

My life has more meaning now,
I live every day, and how!

So the person that you see
Behind the mask, is me.

Hilary Claydon

This poem is published as a tribute to the memory of the late Peter Yardley, a poet who had Parkinson's.

IF YOU GAVE

If you gave
A grain of sand
To an oyster,
With your hand;
And did later
Take away,
A pearl.

Then who can say
What is the thing
That turns a man
Into a king?

Peter Yardley

MY TRUE FEELINGS
(To my friend)

Parkinson's and pain go together it seems.
Some days I grow weaker,
Sometimes the pain will not say goodbye.
My life is ruled by pills.
Why should I bother?
Give me an answer why
One day I am happy, my head high in the sky,
And next day Parkinson's torments me.
Life then can be no fun,
When that happens I don't know which way to run.

I would like to be happy with what time
I have left.
God in heaven I am not brave...
Why have you chosen me?
I have done no harm to anyone
That I can see.

                              Enid Long

Humour

I will never knit dishcloths
No never
No matter what!

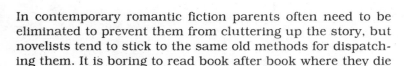

In contemporary romantic fiction parents often need to be eliminated to prevent them from cluttering up the story, but novelists tend to stick to the same old methods for dispatching them. It is boring to read book after book where they die in a car crash. All that's needed is a little imagination.

Ideally, they should be sent as far away as possible. Have them both join the Army, become teachers in Outer Mongolia. Make them guides for treks over the Himalayas, or doctors administering to children in Borneo.

Sometimes, though, the only solution is to kill them off and an influenza epidemic is a good standby, as is a broken leg leading to blood poisoning. In period romances there are all kinds of plagues to fall back on. Even today, cholera is always breaking out somewhere.

Natural disasters can be very upmarket. Daddy could be an explorer who perishes at the North Pole, or is consumed by cannibals or gets buried under the volcano lava. Mummy could have eaten something nasty on a package holiday or fallen off a cruise ship. The trouble with this kind of accident is that you can only dispose of one parent, because to lose them both in such bizarre circumstances would appear too much of a coincidence. Although you *could* get rid of them both if they are in this native bus when a coconut hits the driver, causing him to lose control of the vehicle – dot dot dot.

One death can lead to another. For instance, when Daddy perishes on the polar expedition, Mummy is so crazed with grief she drives off, straight over the nearest cliff. Or perhaps Daddy dives from the liner in a vain attempt to rescue her.

In one of my novels, both parents were marine biologists working in a bathyscope in the Adriatic when an accident occurred. Dad was killed instantly. Mum's lungs were damaged and she died two years later after devoted nursing by the heroine. It only took a small paragraph to explain it all.

In another novel, Dad was thrown from his horse, then Mum remarried and went to live in Spain. How about having Dad involved in a clay-pigeon shooting accident and Mum, heartbroken, going off to nurse lepers?

Parents may be struck by stray golf-balls, tossed by bulls, trampled by elephants, captured by head-hunters. They can fall through glass doors, step on poisonous snakes, interrupt dangerous criminals, be bitten by rabid dogs, given the wrong injection and locked in strong-rooms over the Christmas holidays.

Most accidents happen in the home, so consider chip pans, toadstools and loose mats. The local paper is a trea-sure trove of people fatally falling off ladders, getting into fights or just swimming after a heavy meal.

Having parents die heroically has certain appeal too, such as rescuing an old lady from a smoke-filled bedsit; throwing someone out of the way of a herd of stampeding horses. And think of the opportunities in hang-gliding, snorkeling, shooting the rapids, going on marathons and being missionaries.

The ways and means are endless, so don't let's have any more car crashes. Please.

Joy St.Clair

PARKINSON'S – IF YOU PLEASE

Parkinson's Disease:

      makes you ill at ease
      makes you hard to please
      makes women difficult to squeeze
      makes you weak at the knees
      makes both your feet freeze
      makes it tedious to prune trees
      makes it impossible to catch fleas
      makes your brain start to seize
      makes it tricky to eat peas!

That's Parkinson's – if you please

Howard Stephens

THE YOUTH WITH THE ELEGANT FEET
(Dedicated to C.F. [J])

Whether walking in rain
Or catching a train,
In Winter's cold or Summer's heat,
He's always out,
He's always about,
THE YOUTH WITH THE ELEGANT FEET

He'll be in the park
Till dusk turns to dark
Hoping his friends to meet.
The masses that passes
Admire his chassis,
THE YOUTH WITH THE ELEGANT FEET

If his girl-friend is nigh,
He'll shiver and sigh
Just to give her a little treat,
But if she tries to hold him
She'll have to forego him,
THE YOUTH WITH THE ELEGANT FEET

To be single and free
Is what he likes to be,
To sail an adventurous sea,
To settle down
Would only bring frowns
From THE YOUTH WITH THE ELEGANT FEET

So I wish him luck
And a long, long time
To indulge in his wandering spree,
He will not regret it
Nor ever forget it
THE YOUTH WITH THE ELEGANT FEET!

Ursula Madden

101

MY GRAN'S BOX

My gran collects wooden boxes.
That big one out there in the hall,
The one we all use to sit on,
It's a coffin, shroud, corpse and all.

Her pa brought it home from abroad.
He'd followed the custom out there.
And had Greatgran embalmed
As soon as she stopped breathing air.

Of course, she should have been buried,
But, if he put her deep in the ground,
She threatened she'd come back and haunt him.
So that's why her coffin's around.

Hey. Don't run away. Do stay to tea.
My gran's this world's greatest cook.
We'll play some games and eat our tea
Then we'll open the box so you can look.

                    Janis Priestley

A MOTHER'S EXCUSES
or 'I'M SORRY I HAVEN'T DONE IT BUT...'

Last week was so busy, I knew I'd fail,
I washed the clothes and ironed them too,
And took the money at a jumble sale,
Helped with homework, explained what to do,
Quietened quarrels with stern words and love,
And you hoped I'd do that! Good heavens above.

I tiled the loo and scrubbed the floor.
And rang father's cousin to ask her to tea.
So I baked a cake and, what is more,
Since she is coming, the house has to be
Polished and scrubbed from top to toe
Until all the windows and woodwork glow.

I'm honoured you asked, but I haven't the time.
That rip in the wallpaper, I must repair,
Curtains to wash if the weather stays fine.
And jam to make for the school Autumn Fayre.
Pears to pick and the garden needs weeding
And dozens of animals wanting feeding.

I've to put a new zip in my daughter's jeans
And stitch a fringe round the edge of her skirt.
For if I don't she'll throw one of her scenes.
There's a stain to remove from my husband's shirt
And letters to write and poems as well,
Besides teaching my son the right way to spell.

Then there's the shopping that has to be done.
For food and clothes and garden stuff too.
I feel it's a chore although it's good fun.
But it all takes time and you know that's true.
I have to walk as I haven't a car,
Yes, I do know that it's not very far.

When I get home and have packed it away,
There are always more jobs that I have to do.
A meal to cook or a table to lay,
A broken vase needing mending with glue.
I've holes in the wall to fill with plaster,
It must be done or there'll be a disaster.

Janis Priestley

SAY CHEESE PLEASE

‿᷽᷾᷍‿

SAY CHEESE, PLEASE

and I say no.
Can't make me smile.
Can't make me grin.
I won't say cheese,
I won't begin
to let that smile
under my skin
creep up past
my grinless
chin!

oh, no....
Here it comes.
I feel it sneak
on to my face.
I feel it peek
around my cheek.
I feel it chase
my frown away.
Now my smile
is here to stay.
I guess you win
'cause when you say,

SAY CHEESE, PLEASE

Lynda McKenzie

MY COOKER

Why does it burn, when my back I turn,
Why do I never know,
      the perfect time my cake should need,
When my cook books are there in a row.
I read the instructions, as clear as can be,
I'm beginning to think it must be me,
Sometimes they rise as a good sponge should,
Sometimes they end up like a piece of wood.
The meat looks burnt on the outside,
      but inside it's bloody red,
You mustn't try to do two things at once,
      as my mother always said.
My fruit pies boil over, all into the meat,
But I must admit, the gravy's a treat.
My rice pudding should be all milky and sweet,
But it's tasting of onions and just like concrete.
It's true my cooker is getting old,
      and, like me, doesn't always do as it's told.
But the oven I was told to fill to the limit,
I do till I can't get any more in it.
Perhaps it doesn't like to be full as can be,
      Neither do I,
So why cook all this lot, just for me?

                          M.K. Brooke

A PD RHYME

What rhymes with Parkinson's Disease?

The whisper of a summer breeze,
A distant sail on silver seas,
The furry coats of bumble bees,
Autumn – the colours of the trees,
Or even celery and cheese!

I hope such pleasant thoughts as these
Can sometimes bring a little ease
To those with Parkinson's Disease.

Joan New

THANK YOU

(All staff on A4)

For scooping me up off the floor
Time and time again.
For being kind when I was low
And keeping me quite sane.
For putting up with all the stupid
Things that I have done.
(The "launching of the lifeboat" when
Bathtime became quite fun!)
It's great to know that someone cares
And helps one on life's way,
With cheery words and helping hands,
Encouragement each day.
I hope I haven't harrassed *you*
Or caused *you* too much pain.
Don't heave a sigh and wave goodbye;
(You *might* see me again!)

Pamela Phillips

AN OUTING

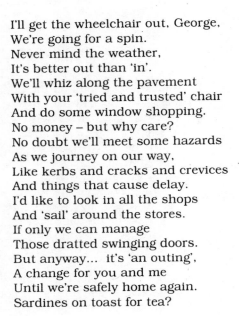

I'll get the wheelchair out, George,
We're going for a spin.
Never mind the weather,
It's better out than 'in'.
We'll whiz along the pavement
With your 'tried and trusted' chair
And do some window shopping.
No money – but why care?
No doubt we'll meet some hazards
As we journey on our way,
Like kerbs and cracks and crevices
And things that cause delay.
I'd like to look in all the shops
And 'sail' around the stores.
If only we can manage
Those dratted swinging doors.
But anyway... it's 'an outing',
A change for you and me
Until we're safely home again.
Sardines on toast for tea?

Margaret Randall

WHAT A NERVE

I will never knit dishcloths

No never
No matter what!

It's a diabolical liberty

To take my creativity

And then

Not asking

What I think

Plunge it..... in the sink.

Vina Curren

PLEASE PHONE BACK

I called with a prayer

You did not hear me

Oh God get an answer phone.

Vina Curren

THE EXPLETIVE PLEA

What will I do now I am past my prime and in decline?
What will I do when my body disobeys my brain,
When my arm shakes, my emotions are raw
And tears flow, when dark clouds loom
And all of me is doom and gloom,
What will I do?

Let me tell you what I do.

When I drop things, I swear!
When I shake, I curse!
And the shake is no worse for a curse.

When I cry, then I am cleansed,
Tears flow, tensions go... but slow,
And so...
I treat myself to flowers, fill all my vases and create
My own personal Kew Gardens.

When in town I visit M&S and buy a prawn sandwich,
Which I eat sitting on a bench
In the precinct and view the passing parade and think...
Life's a sod!
But still I put my prawny, sticky, shaky hand, my trust
In God.
And refuse to apologise to those who do not understand
That prayers can be heartfelt pleas expressed in expletives.
When in the shower I sometimes think
Perhaps this dratted nuisance might just disappear
            down the sink.

But it's a game you see that we all have played,
We call it 'Let's Pretend'.
We confidently bury our heads and say
'It will never happen to me'.
The poet said, 'Ask not for whom the bell tolls, it tolls for
thee'.

So if you can grab the rope and hold on tight
You might say OK, what the hell:
If this is my bell
I will decide,
I will say... what tune I play.

                                    Vina Curren

111

HELP

I promise to live my life, my whole life,
And every day of my life... to the full
So help me God!
I will enjoy more, forgive and forget more,
Anticipate the future, whatever it may hold,
And not regret the past, the frittered moments.
I will spoil myself, and not feel guilty,
I will be gentle with myself,
I will be who I want to be,
          and not what others expect me to be.
I will have my hair done more often
And paint my toenails.
I will splash myself with my most expensive perfume...
Before I do the ironing!
I will soak in the bath for two hours, with a coffee liqueur,
          a thousand bubbles and a 'who done it',
          and admire my crinkly skin.
I will eat Black Forest Gateaux for breakfast...
          muesli makes my jaws ache!
I will fill my arms... all the way up
          with free squirts of perfume in Boots.
And accept all free samples of cheese and wine in Tesco.
I will slide down the Great Orme on my bottom
And not worry about the grass stains.
And (furtively) zoom down shiny bannister rails
          in posh hotels –
It will save my legs.
I will grow old disgracefully!!
So I promise to live this life,
          this whole life, and every bit of this life.
So help me God... because it might not be easy.

Vina Curren

OVERHEARD AT THE MARKET
(spoken in a Suffolk dialect)

How you gitting on me old mate?
I'm nearly past me sell by date.
The missus ain't bin none too well,
Can't git her wind and her ankles swell.
Lovely weather, we can't complain,
Me taters could do with a damn good rain.
What do you think of that Gorbachev bloke?
He's trying to sell us a pig in a poke.
I don't like this poll tax, it ain't at all fair,
And what about this cow disease scare?
Well I must be going, see you old pal,
Me missus will think I've got another old gal!
Cheerio bor.

Hubert William Stuteley

ANGLIAN WATER MAN

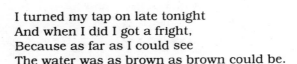

I turned my tap on late tonight
And when I did I got a fright,
Because as far as I could see
The water was as brown as brown could be.

Such murky water, what a disgrace.
Anglian Water had egg on its face.

My neighbour, June, called around,
Said her chicken had turned brown –
When she washed it inside
Brown gunge came out, so hard to hide.

I said that I would telephone
And I was not alone.
Other people had rung too
To complain, like people do.

You said a man would come along
To see what had indeed gone wrong.
You said a pipe might have burst
Or something else which might be worse.

As a Londoner, I was sure
That I'd heard it all before.
I didn't suppose a man would come,
But I was very wrong, my chum.

An Anglian Water van appeared
And the dishiest man I'd seen in years.

Now I must stop to explain
That gasmen I have found quite plain.
BT men don't fire a spark,
Electricity men leave me in the dark.

Anglian Water may well be brown,
But who cares, when men like him come round?

His ID card shown at the door,
His shoes removed to protect my floor.
Into my kitchen he made his way,
He was so tasty it made my day.

Now those who know me very well
Will know I'm fussy, what the hell.
There are not men, young or old,
Who turn my head, it must be told.

But this young man, whose name was Mark,
Enjoyed the banter, it was a lark.
So Anglian Water, I thank you,
For sending water brown, not blue.

Without the gunge I would not have met
This young man, who was such a pet.

If I were younger, not forty five,
And also if I were more alive,
A toy boy I'd get sent around
And from Anglian Water, he'd be found.

                    Hilary Claydon

115

SCOTT

I write now of my plumber,
A young man, name of Scott.
Since I moved into my new house,
He's been there quite a lot.

He's plumbed my dishwasher in,
He's done my taps as well.
He's even put a shower in,
So now I do not smell.

He's charming and quite tasty,
And if I were not so old,
I think I'd set my cap at him;
I think I'd be quite bold.

He has a twinkle in his eye.
He smiles at you when you walk by.
And when he works he grunts a lot,
Especially when it's very hot.

He listens to my poems
As he stands there in my bath.
I must add that he's working,
But we really have a laugh.

Now Scott, who is the plumber,
Of this poet 'Hil',
There's only one thing wrong with him –
He sends me in a bill.

Hilary Claydon

I'M ALWAYS IN A HURRY!

I'm always in a hurry,
Like a frantic Tom and Jerry –
I'm always in a hurry, yet I don't get very far.
It's like dashing for the last train,
Or driving in the fast lane
When you only have a little pedal-car!

I think I know the trouble,
'Cos my mind works at the double,
But my feet don't seem to really want to know.
We can't communicate – though I try to indicate
In which direction I am wanting them to go!

So if you see my puppeteer,
Please say that I'm still here
But it's getting very clear,
Some strings are broke, you see.
If they'll send some men to mend 'em,
So I can superintend 'em,
Then I can recommend 'em
To some other folk like me !!

Bert Tolfrey

117

NON-SCHOOL UNIFORM

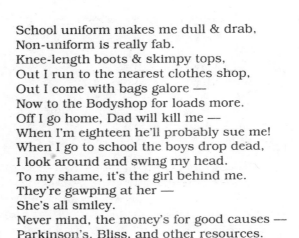

School uniform makes me dull & drab,
Non-uniform is really fab.
Knee-length boots & skimpy tops,
Out I run to the nearest clothes shop,
Out I come with bags galore —
Now to the Bodyshop for loads more.
Off I go home, Dad will kill me —
When I'm eighteen he'll probably sue me!
When I go to school the boys drop dead,
I look around and swing my head.
To my shame, it's the girl behind me.
They're gawping at her —
She's all smiley.
Never mind, the money's for good causes —
Parkinson's, Bliss, and other resources.

Tara Vasudevan

Seasons

Words fail to utter your exquisite beauty,
Did you drop from another planet
                    where snow is made?

SNOW

When I woke the world was white,
White as white, clear and bright.
All the world was quiet too,
Under its blanket of pristine whiteness,
As though its beauty rendered speechless
The people wondering at its brightness.

Sylvia Davidson

WINTER FLOWERING CHERRY

You've got it all wrong you silly tree.
This is winter.
Nine degrees of frost last night
And this morning, what do I see
Breaking open from tiny buds?
The palest of pale pink flowers
Tumbling down your leaf-bare branches,
Clusters of tiny rose-hued showers.
Remember my surprise the first time
I gazed incredulously
At your inane absurdity?
That now gives me such delight.
Every year as November dies,
First one bud opens then a cluster
Until, little tree you're dusted
With petals of fragrant blossom,
A bride in an embroidered gown
Of silken pearls on Limerick lace.

Janis Priestley

A VERY MERRY CHRISTMAS

Santa came down the chimney and cursed quietly to himself as he put his foot on to some coals which were still hot.

"It's bad enough being expected to squeeze oneself down these miniature modern chimneys without burning one's feet at the bottom!" he muttered crossly to himself.

He brushed some soot from the white fur at the back of his suit and stepped firmly out of the fireplace and into the room.

"Thank heavens," he murmured softly, regarding with pleasure the bottle of sherry, glass and mincepie which had been left for him. He downed one glass hastily and ate the mincepie. Gleefully he poured himself another glass and looked at the label on the bottle.

"Harvey's Bristol Cream, my, but it's good."

A third glass followed the second, and a fourth the third. Tipsily he reached into his sack and brought out the first four presents he found and dropped them on the floor near the fire. On his way back up the chimney, he burped and hiccuped as his body, wormlike, stretched and contracted all the way up the narrow aperture. Climbing out of the chimney, he wobbled precariously on the ridge of the roof, drunkenly attempting to climb back into his sleigh. Successful at last, Rudolf looked at him and snorted his disgust, took the vague flap of the reins to mean "go", and leapt into the air on the way to the next port of call.

Santa made his way down this chimney, in a state of inebriation which was insufficient to prevent him enjoying the large glass of sherry left especially for him. Not forgetting his duties, he carefully selected three large parcels and arranged them decoratively against the back of the sofa – before deciding to investigate the contents of the sideboard. It was with considerable satisfaction that he found and drained half a bottle of Emva Cream Sherry.

At the bottom of the third chimney, Santa found something different left in a glass for him. He sniffed cautiously. No-one had left him anything but sherry or an occasional coffee for centuries. He tasted it gingerly, liked it, drank it and developed a taste for rum. Once more he left presents as was his wont, and left; almost collapsing in a heap halfway up the chimney; but the thought of having to start off at the bottom again gave him the necessary incentive to reach the top.

By now he had a great deal of incentive to continue his work and he almost fell down the chimney in his eagerness to reach the bottom. Set on the hearth, by a properly raked out fire, was a large piece of Christmas cake, a mug and a vacuum flask. He unscrewed the top and poured the steaming brown liquid into the mug. The hot, sweet coffee steadied his sodden brain for a moment and he looked into his sack for more gifts. Leaving these suitably placed, his befuddled brain registered that these were the last that he had. What was he to do? Then, with great relief, he saw, arranged neatly under the Christmas tree, a new supply. He packed these, gratefully, into his sack and left once more via the chimney.

All this going up and down chimneys might be in the contract, but the limit was reached when one got stuck behind three gas fires in a row. However, very fairly he left the right number of presents behind each fire.

Six houses, five sherries, four mincepies, one coffee and two slices of Christmas cake later, Santa was no longer able to go up and down the chimneys. So he resorted to the expediency of dropping the presents down the chimneys and hoping for the best. By now, all he wanted to do was to go to bed and he began to drowse off between each house. Fortunately he remembered that his sleigh was jammed full of gifts he'd brought with him; even so, he contemplated gratefully the thoughtfulness of those people who had left him some to take. As dawn began to break, Rudolf set a course for home, well aware that Santa was too drunk to be in charge of the sleigh.

§

Next morning, at each of the houses that Santa had visited, there was a mixture of anger and gloom. The gifts that Santa had so carefully distributed were in no way suitable for their recipients. Eighteen year old Brian's reaction to his Fisher Price Play Centre was, in his father's views, a trifle excessive. Puritan Eleanor's reaction to a year's subscription to Playboy magazine could only be described as hysterical and an early divorce nearly ensued. At the Tobin's house, Margaret and Daniel had called in the police about

123

the theft of their gifts and were being extremely coy about telling the increasingly irate Inspector what had actually been stolen and kept whispering down his ear.

The Gas Board, called out to a series of exploding gas fires, were at a loss to explain the ragged relics of freshly wrapped gifts, which they had found behind the fires and which were the cause of the explosions.

Only one little girl was happy. Her family were so poor that she had been told that there would be no presents this Christmas. To her delight, Santa had left her an enormous blue teddy.

Early in the New Year, Mr Donaghue called a meeting of the residents in the locality. What was to be done? Such an invasion of one's privacy had to be prevented. It was decided to approach a burglar alarm company to see if they could get a massive reduction in price for a bulk order to fit up all the houses in the road. That should put paid to the old reprobate, they decided, nodding agreement among themselves.

Such an agreement was duly made and put into motion. So, by the following Christmas, all the houses on that part of Santa's route were fitted with heat and movement scanners. Everyone was sure that there would be no more trouble. But they had reckoned without Santa, whose eyesight, let's face it, had been questionable for a least one hundred and twenty years. Besides which, if you wanted to warn Santa that your house had been fitted with a burglar alarm, it would be wiser to put the little red box on the roof of your house rather than on the side. However, since it had been snowing, even that might not have helped.

Santa arrived, a warm glow of anticipation causing him to step out of his sleigh with alacrity and slip down the first chimney as if he were on a slide at a children's playground. He barely had time to discover that no sherry had been left for him, when the horrific siren went off and he shot back up the chimney and into his sleigh as if he were being chased by a herd of buffaloes.

It happened again and again, until Santa, sober but breathless, said to Rudolf:

"Enough is enough. Tomorrow I shall resign, or try to get made redundant. Yes, that would be better. The redundancy payment I should get after over seven hundred years should come to quite a tidy sum."

So Santa and Rudolf went home to get an early night for

the first Christmas since the blackout during the war, when they had been unable to go out because the ARP wardens kept complaining about the sleigh lights and bells.

All the residents of Little Hassle who had been shaken awake by the reverberant siren promptly decided that maybe a Santa disaster was less traumatic than being woken at night by the burglar alarms. So next Christmas they planned to leave them switched off for the night.

On Boxing Day, Santa went to see the North Pole Management Committee to explain his predicament. The Committee said that, under the circumstances, and bearing in mind that the notion of a free gift at Christmas was not now economically viable, especially in view of the escalating costs (even though they had for years bought all the gifts in the summer sales), if Santa were prepared to accept a large, no, sizable, cheque as redundancy payment, they would go bankrupt. Then they could open up a new business scheme called, perhaps, 'Father Christmas in Stores PLC'. This would, in their view, be more practical and more of an on-going situation.

Santa was delighted. He dropped all his remaining Christmas presents down the chimney of the little girl to whom he'd given the blue teddy the year before, gave all his reindeer their freedom in the Tundra, though Rudolf wouldn't leave him as they'd been together for too long.

§

After a lot of consideration, Santa decided against buying up Guinness or Distillers' Company Limited, though sorely tempted. Instead, he bought a post office store in a remote village in Wales. Everyone there just thinks of him as a kindly old man with a host of stories and a bottomless experience of life. But every so often, on a clear, crisp Christmas Eve, he and Rudolf take the old sleigh for a run through the sky for old times' sake and sometimes, if you listen quietly, you can hear the jingle of sleigh bells as a shadow slips across the moon.

Janis Priestley

THE QUEUE

Christmas, in our house, usually starts at about 7.00 pm on 24th December. The main reason for this is that I refuse, on principle, to take any serious notice of 'High Street Tinsel-Time' and all its accompanying hysteria, before the beginning of December at the very least. I take up a dignified stance on the side-lines, observing the proceedings with a detached air, while firmly resisting any attempts by over-zealous shop-keepers to draw me in. It happens every succeeding Christmas and this last one was no exception. It invariably gets to the middle of the month before I start making any serious effort to begin the 'necessaries'. Usually, it works out alright, and I am still able to get what I intended to get – or, if not quite that, then something very similar which serves the purpose equally well. However, this year I finally got my come-uppance, having, as usual, deluded myself into the belief that most people would have already done their shopping, and therefore queues would be vastly reduced. How wrong can you be? They were still bursting at the seams and remained so, right up until the last available moment on Christmas Eve. Consequently, many of the late shoppers in Wigan and Southport were able to go home with a ready-made excuse as to why they were so late back. I could almost see them relating – half-amused, half-irritated – to their wide-eyed, hungry and disgruntled families, the story of how '...this stupid woman further up in the queue steadfastly refused to move either up or out of the queue, insisting that her feet were stuck to the floor! Did you ever hear such nonsense! Several of us had seen her a few moments before, behaving perfectly normally. Honestly, the lengths that some people will go to get to the front of a queue is incredible! Of course I blame the Social Services. They shouldn't allow those people out of their institutions on their own. They can't cope and they're a menace to serious shoppers.'

Feeling somewhat deflated and highly frustrated, I made my long, slow journey home, wistfully wishing that my Fairy Godmother would get her act together and turn me into a beautiful Cinderella instead of into a pumpkin!

When I got home, I too related the story, just as it had happened, to my own family. They listened with genuine interest, and that subtle blend of sympathy and humour which seems to be a genetic trait in our family. As I gradually found myself able to unwind and relax in the warm, comforting atmosphere which their response had created, and laugh with them at the amusing situation their comments conjured up in our minds, I was reminded of the words of a song from Andrew Lloyd Webber's *Aspects of Love* entitled 'Love Changes Everything', and I sent up a silent prayer of thanksgiving to God in appreciation of all that I had. After all – isn't *giving* what Christmas is all about?

Love can turn your world around
And that love will last forever!

Ursula Madden

SNOWDROPS AT CANDLEMAS

We hail your birth, February Fair Maids!
Dressed in your white, three petalled capes,
Revealing green daintily embroidered skirts,
Protecting from the blast your precious gold within,
As you await the Moon's summons to peal at Candlemas.

Your long supporting stem provides a canopy rare,
Over your delicate neck from which you hang
Bent in adoration for the *Feast* of Candlemas
Acknowledging the Purity of the Mother of our Lord.

When cold grey clouds leaned heavily on the hills,
And the snow and the ice were one with the deep rich soil,
When we mortals imagined all was dead,
You bravely broke through with your message of new life.

Words fail to utter your exquisite beauty,
Did you drop from another planet where snow is made?
Or from Paradise, where pains and sorrows cease?
And tears and regrets are replaced by healing
And Joy remains, and Peace.

You look like tiny lanterns of incandescent light
Made pure by the sun's fiery blaze of glory,
Before you were presented to Mother Earth
To share life's rhythms and its transience.

You come to us near the dawn of each new year.
Your presence, a sign that Spring is drawing near,
Are you, perchance, the tears of our guardian angels
Calling us to Purity from our earthly world?

Even 'tho the winds and snows are fierce,
Your short visit year by year gives us hope
As you push your way upwards through the frozen earth,
Bringing light and new life to dull wintry days.

Last year's dead leaves, ash – oak – beech – lime...
Now laid to rest, after their battering by autumn's storms,
Matured by a whole range of sun, rain and frost
Filtered through to you their life-giving wine and dew.

And you too will soon lie down to rest,
When your life's tapestry is done,
But before that day dawns, you will
In your white petalled humility
Lead in glorious array the flowers of all the earth.

Flowers ablaze in every colour and design
Daffodils, lilies, violets, roses...
All flowers from bushes and trees,
Each completing their life's cycle.

As their time comes round and their leaves and petals drop
Into the soil, they release to you their life-giving wine
That you once more may reveal to our dull earthy minds,
Our Creator's Purity and Loveliness Divine.

J. Summers

PARKINSON'S CHRISTMAS THOUGHT

Now Christmas time is here once more
    When snowflakes pile against my door,
Yet I shall not with cold conspire,
    But in my veins retain the fire,
Those very flames that fuel my life
    Warm through my soul, ignoring strife,
For at this precious hour I see
    True gentle folk still shielding me.

So gathered as we are this day,
    Let us give thought before we pray,
To other souls with lesser ways
    And to their pain in darker days,
For even now their grief remains
    Encouraged by life's bitter rains,
Whilst in my heart I truly feel
    The need to live stays strong and real.

Let us refrain from counting cost
    Or adding scores of all skills lost,
But pledge our scorn at vile disease
    By smiling when and where we please,
So much is left that I hold dear,
    Like splendid seasons every year,
Fresh miracles of early dawn
    Leaves me so glad that I was born.

Friends' tender care, a baby's kiss,
        A woman's smile with lasting bliss,
Rich fruit trees grown in fertile earth,
        All gifts from God for holy birth,
Sweet joyous smell of growing flowers,
        Our perfect rest in sleeping hours,
The taste of pure clean English air
        And all it means, just being there.

When gifts of clay are aged and gone,
        Still Nature's work shall linger on,
Despite my sad and slow decline,
        These joys from God shall still be mine,
For I have loved this life so much
        Since first I learned to see and touch,
Though sickness stays despised by me,
        More precious years are sure to be.

                                    F. Ball

131

LORDS OF SPRING

Look at the horse chestnuts!
Overdoing it again
hogging the glory
thrusting up their proud spires
creamy-white with blood-red cuff
rose-pink dappled brown
and if this were not enough
ostentatiously scarlet
aristocrats at a glance
haughty and pointed
never giving the other trees a chance.
They do it every year –
what are they trying to prove?
That each is king,
a majestic lord of spring?
But the limes were never contenders
nor the oaks
and every sycamore surrenders
vain chestnuts!
Is all this showing off
really necessary?

Joy St. Clair

Animals

and other creatures

Jonah, the psychedelic whale,
Fell in love with a garden snail.

THE PSYCHEDELIC WHALE

Jonah, the psychedelic whale,
Fell in love with a garden snail.
From the start his love was blighted.
Sad to say it was unrequited.

Janis Priestley

SEAHORSES

WAVES
AND BREAKERS
TUMBLING, RIPPLING
ACROSS THE SEA,
SMASH THEM–
SELVES TO
PIECES, ON
THE SHORE,
IN FRONT OF ME.
WHEN ANGRY TEMPESTS
BLOW, WILD HORSES
OUT OF REACH PLUNGE   AND
TOSS SNOWY HEADS AND   RACE
TOWARDS THE BEACH.   WHITE
CRESTED SEAHORSES,
PRANCING TOWARDS
THE LAND. EACH
STRIVING TO
BE FIRST
TO COL–
LAPSE
UPON
THE
STR
AND.
SEA
HORSES
SEAHOR–
SES.

Janis Priestley

CAT OF THE NIGHT

Prowl, cat, prowl through the jet-black night,
With brain alert and dark eyes bright.
A hunter's face with a whiskered gleam.
Orion's child, malevolent machine.

A banshee's scream, a moon-curdled purr.
An eldritch creature with frightened fur.
So, go, hunter, go. Fiendish cat-sprite.
For cats are lords of the earth at night.

With brazen eyes, return at dawn,
To sit and purr with claws indrawn
As if the night-hunt had merely been
An idle thought, an enchanted dream.

Janis Priestley

THE SPIDER

On leaving the bathroom, just going out,
I glimpsed a spider by the water spout,
So turning round I began to stare
As I was surprised to see it there,
For it came to me as quite a shock
As it was early morning, about 7 o'clock.
I moved forward taking one big stride
And he was in the bath walking up the side,
I thought of him being on my skin,
It would have made my blood turn thin,
So I ran some water in a mug
And tried to coax him down the plug.
After two attempts he finally went
So I felt my effort had been well spent,
For had I bathed with him on my back,
I'd probably have had a heart attack.

Howard Stephens

MY CAT

I have a lovely cat called Smudge
He's long haired, black and white
He never ever bears a grudge
And neither does he fight.

He has a small but pretty face
With a character all his own
And when he is around the place
I don't feel I'm alone.

He has a very big appetite
And loves a plate of fish
For he could eat this day or night
As it's his favourite dish.

Often when he's had his food
He acts just like a sop
I fuss him when he's in the mood
He lays there till I stop.

Then when he goes outside the house
He likes to have a run
He'll chase a bird or catch a mouse
And have tremendous fun.

Later when he comes indoors
He'll be so nice and sweet
He'll have a wash and lick his paws
Then lay down by my feet.

I know now that I love my cat
And all his funny ways
For nothing else will change the fact
I'll love him all my days.

Howard Stephens